Thai

at your Fingertips

Other titles in this series

Thai

at your fingertips

compiled by

LEXUS

with

Manat Chitakasem
and
David Smyth

ROUTLEDGE

London

First published 1988
Reprinted in 1990 and 1991
by Routledge
11 New Fetter Lane, London EC4P 4EE

Set by Morton Word Processing Ltd, Scarborough
and Computype, West Drayton
and printed in the British Isles
by The Guernsey Press Co. Ltd
Guernsey, Channel Islands

British Library Cataloguing in Publication Data

Thai at your fingertips. – (Fingertips).
1. Thai language – Conversation and phrase books
I. Lexus   II. Chitakasem, Manas
III. Smyth, David, *1954* –   IV. Series
495.9'13421   PL4163.5

ISBN 0–415–00237–0

Contents

Introduction

Thai differs from English and other more familiar European languages in two major areas: firstly, it is a tonal language, which means that the meaning of a syllable is determined by the pitch at which it is pronounced, and secondly, it has none of the complicated verb and noun endings which we tend to associate with foreign language learning from our school days. This leads to two commonly held misconceptions about the Thai language, namely that you have to be musically gifted to speak the language, and that it has no grammar. Although neither of these claims is correct, Westerners nevertheless often find that considerable effort is needed to produce the correct tone of a word, while the grammar (see page 95) remains relatively easy.

TONES

Thai has five different tones: mid-tone (no tone mark given), high-tone (´), low-tone (`), falling-tone (^) and rising-tone (ˇ). Thus, in theory, (although fortunately rather rarely in practice) what to the Westerner appears to be one word can have any one of five meanings. For example:

mai	(mid-tone)	ไมล์	mile
mái	(high-tone)	ไม้	(question word)
mài	(low-tone)	ใหม่	new
mâi	(falling-tone)	ไหม้	burn
mǎi	(rising-tone)	ไหม	silk

The tone of a Thai word is, then, clearly as much an integral part of the word as the consonant and vowel sounds, something the Englishman, who used to exclaim in frustration, 'I can remember the word, but not the damn tone', had really failed to appreciate. For this reason, Thai script equivalents of words in this section have been given so that you can ask a Thai speaker to demonstrate the tonal differences for you; if possible, try to record a Thai saying these words, so that you can refer back to them.

(i) *Mid-tone* (as in **tum** ทำ to do).

This is best thought of as being the speaker's normal voice pitch. Be careful not to let your voice trail off at the end of the syllable, as is the natural tendency when we pronounce English words in isolation. Here are some other words pronounced with mid-tone which you might ask a Thai speaker to record for you:

mah	มา	come	**nai**	ใน	in
bpai	ไป	go	**koon**	คุณ	you
dee	ดี	good	**gin**	กิน	eat

(ii) *High-tone* (as in **náhm** น้ำ water).

The voice has to be pitched higher than normal, although this does not mean slipping into a falsetto voice or soaring like a soprano! There are plenty of Thai men with deep bass voices who manage to produce high tones without any problem. This is because tones are not fixed like musical notes, but are relative to each other. The crucial factor is the 'shape' or 'direction' of the tone, rather than the absolute pitch.

Some common words with high-tones are:

rót	รถ	car	**lék**	เล็ก	little
rúk	รัก	love	**púk**	พัก	stay
láir-o	แล้ว	already	**chét**	เช็ด	wipe

(iii) *Low-tone* (as in **tòok** ถูก cheap).

The voice is pitched slightly below the normal level.

bài	บ่าย	afternoon	**jàhk**	จาก	from
yàhk	อยาก	want to	**gài**	ไก่	chicken
dtòrp	ตอบ	reply	**nèung**	หนึ่ง	one

(iv) *Falling-tone* (as in **mâi** ไม่ not).

The voice starts at a fairly high pitch and falls dramatically. Westerners tend to find this the most difficult tone to reproduce, often producing an insufficiently distinct fall, and making it difficult for Thais to distinguish from mid-tone words. Perhaps the best way of thinking of the falling tone in Thai is to imagine a conversation between two characters, the first being slightly hard of hearing:

A: Are you going?
B: Yes.
A: Pardon?
B: (*louder*) Yes!
A: Sorry, I still didn't quite catch that.
B: YES!

B's final 'YES!' will almost certainly have been a very good Thai falling tone; the Westerner learning Thai has to learn to make that sharp fall, without raising the volume of his voice as B doubtless did. Some common Thai words with falling tones are:

chôrp	ชอบ	like	**dtôrng**	ต้อง	must
mâhk	มาก	much	**kâhng nâh**	ข้างหน้า	in front
dâi	ได้	can	**yâhk**	ยาก	difficulty

(v) *Rising-tone* (as in **kǒr ...?** ขอ may I...?)

The rising-tone in Thai corresponds very closely to the intonation we use when asking questions, as for example when we say 'Really?' Further examples are:

sŏrng	สอง	two	kăi	ขาย	sell
săhm	สาม	three	mŏr	หมอ	doctor
lăi	หลาย	several	sĕe	สี	colour

It is worth bearing in mind (a) that falling tones rise to a fairly high pitch in order to achieve a sufficiently dramatic fall and (b) that rising tones drop to a fairly low pitch before rising.

MALE/FEMALE

You will see that options for male and female speakers are given in the English-Thai section of this text. These are:

pŏm (chún)	I/me
krúp (kâ)	polite particle

The difference is that the option given in brackets is the form that should be used by female speakers. For more on this see the grammar section, pages 101 and 110.

Pronunciation Guide

The Thai in this book has been written in a system which tries to make it as straightforward as possible for an English-speaker to pronounce.

There are some sounds which are quite unlike anything that exists in English words. For some of the items in this pronunciation guide we have given a word containing the Thai script for the relevant sound so that you can ask a Thai to pronounce them out loud for you.

Some comments on the pronunciation:

CONSONANTS

bp	ปัด	a short sharp 'p' (don't actually pronounce the 'b')
dt	ตา	a short sharp 't' (don't actually pronounce the 'd')
j		as in 'jam'
g		as in 'gun' or 'get'
ng		as in 'sing'

Note that when an 'r' occurs at the end of a syllable and the next syllable begins with a vowel, as in the word **ler-ee**, the 'r' is not sounded. Note also that when the consonants 'k', 'p' and 't' occur at the end of a word the sound is not released, although the mouth is positioned for making the appropriate sound. It will sound at first as if these consonants are·not being pronounced at all. Try to listen to a Thai saying:

râhk	ราก
râhp	ราบ
râht	ราช

VOWELS

a		as in 'ago'
e		as in 'when'
i		as in 'bin'
o		as in 'on'
u		as in 'run'
ah		as in 'father'
ai		as in 'Thai'
air		as in 'hair'
ao		as in 'Mao Tse-Tung'
ay		as in 'pay'
ee		as in 'fee'
er		as in 'number'
er-ee	เคย	don't pronounce the 'r'

eu	กืน	this is similar to the English sound of repugnance usually represented as 'ugh'
ew		as in 'pew'
oh		as in 'go'
oo		as in 'boot'
oo		as in 'book'
oy		as in 'boy'

Notes:

1. Many Thais are unable to produce an 'r' sound at the beginning of a word, and substitute an 'l' instead. For example:

   a-rai? (what?) becomes **a-lai?**

   Thais who can produce an initial 'r' frequently pronounce it as a rolled 'r'.

2. In Bangkok Thai, when two consonants occur at the beginning of a word, the second sound is frequently omitted. For example:

   bplah (fish) becomes **bpah**
   gra-jòk (mirror) becomes **ga-jòk**

3. In Bangkok Thai, words beginning with a 'kw' sound are sometimes pronounced as if they began with an 'f' instead. For example:

   kwǎh (right) becomes **fǎh**
   kwahm sòok (happiness) becomes **fahm sòok**

English-Thai

A

a (*per*) lá; **20 baht a bottle** kòo-ut lá yêe-sìp bàht; *see page 95*

about (*approximately*) bpra-mahn; **about 25** bpra-mahn yêe-sìp-hâh; **about 6 o'clock** bpra-mahn hòk mohng; **is the manager about?** pôo-jùt-gahn yòo mái?; **I was just about to leave** pŏm (chún) gum-lung ja bpai dĕe-o née; **how about a drink?** dèum a-rai mái?

above kâhng-bon; **above the village** ler-ee mòo-bâhn bpai nòy

abroad dtàhng bpra-tâyt

abscess fĕe

absolutely: **it's absolutely perfect** yôrt jing jing; **you're absolutely right** kOOn tòok bpĕng; **absolutely!** nâir-norn!

absorbent cotton sŭm-lee

accelerator kun rêng

accept rúp

accident OO-bùt-dti-hàyt; **there's been an accident** mee OO-bùt-dti-hàyt; **sorry, it was an accident** kŏr-tôht mâi dâi dtûng jai

accommodation(s) têe púk; **we need accommodation(s) for four** rao dtôrng-gahn têe púk sŭm-rùp sèe kon

accurate tòok-dtôrng

ache: **I have an ache here** bpòo-ut dtrong nêe; **it aches** bpòo-ut

across: **across the street** ta-nŏn fùng dtrong kâhm

actor núk sa-dairng chai

actress núk sa-dairng yĭng

adapter (*electrical*) krêu-ung bprairng fai fáh

address têe-yòo; **what's your address?** kOOn púk yòo têe-năi?

address book sa-mòot têe-yòo

admission: **how much is admission?** kâh pàhn bpra-dtoo tâo-rài?

adore: **I adore ...** (*this country, this food etc*) pŏm (chún) chôrp ... mâhk

adult pôo-yài

advance: **I'll pay in advance** pŏm (chún) ja jài lôo-ung nâh

advertisement gahn kôh-sa-nah

advise: **what would you advise?** kOOn ja náir-num a-rai?

aerogramme jòt-măi ah-gàht

aeroplane krêu-ung bin

affluent rŏo răh

afraid: **I'm afraid of snakes** pŏm (chún) gloo-a ngoo; **don't be afraid** yàh gloo-a ná; **I'm not afraid** pŏm (chún) mâi gloo-a; **I'm afraid I can't help you** sĕe-a jai têe chôo-ay mâi dâi; **I'm afraid so** róo-sèuk wâh châi; **I'm afraid not** róo-sèuk wâh mâi châi

after lŭng; **after 9 p.m.** lŭng săhm tôom; **after you** chern gòrn

afternoon bài; **in the afternoon** dtôrn bài; **good afternoon** sa-wùt dee krúp (kâ); **this afternoon** bài née

aftershave yah tah lŭng gohn nòo-ut

aftersun cream yah tah lŭng àhp dàirt

afterwards pai lŭng

again èek

against (*the wall*) dùt gùp

age ah-yóo; **under age** ah-yóo mâi tĕung; **not at my age!** mâi dâi! gàir láir-o; **it takes ages** sĕe-a way-lah nahn; **I haven't been here for ages** pŏm (chún) mâi dâi mah têe nêe sĕe-a dtûng nahn

agency ay-yên

aggressive dòo-rái

ago: a year ago bpee têe láir-o;
it wasn't long ago mâi nahn mah
née

agony: it's agony jèp to-ra-mahn

agree (*with sb, sth*) hĕn dôo-ay; do you
agree with me? hĕn dôo-ay mái?;

agreed! dtòk-long láir-o; the food
doesn't agree with me ah-hăhn mâi
tòok bpàhk

AIDS rôhk-ayd

air ah-gàht; by air tahng ah-gàht

air-conditioner krêu-ung air, krêu-
ung bprùp ah-gàht

air-conditioned bus rót air, rót
bprùp ah-gàht

air-conditioned room hôrng air,
hôrng bprùp ah-gàht

air-conditioning krêu-ung air, krêu-
ung bprùp ah-gàht

air hostess air hóht-tet

airmail: by airmail doy-ee tahng ah-
gàht

airmail envelope sorng jòt-măi ah-
gàht

airplane krêu-ung bin

airport sa-năhm bin

airport bus rót sa-năhm bin

airport tax pah-sĕe sa-năhm bin

air-sick mao krêu-ung bin

alarm clock nah-li-gah bplòok

alcohol (*drink*) lâo

alcoholic: is it alcoholic? bpen lâo
mái?

alive mee chee-wít yòo; is he still
alive? káo yung mee chee-wít yòo
mái?

all: all the hotels rohng-rairm túng
mòt; all my friends pêu-un tóok
kon; all my money ngern túng mòt;
all of it túng mòt; all of them
(*people*) tóok kon; (*things*) túng mòt;
all right (*well*) sa-bai dee; I'm all
right pŏm (chún) sa-bai dee; that's
all mòt láir-o, sèt láir-o; it's all
changed bplèe-un bpai mòt; thank
you — not at all kòrp-koon krúp
(kâ) — ʼâi bpen rai

allergic: I'm allergic to ... pŏm

(chún) páir ...

allergy rôhk-páir

all-inclusive rôo-um túng mòt

allowed a-nóo-yâht; is ... allowed? ...
dâi mái?; is smoking allowed? sòop
boo-rèe dâi mái?; I'm not allowed
to eat salt mŏr hâhm mâi hâi gin
gleu-a

almost gèu-up

alone kon dee-o; are you alone?
kOon yòo kon dee-o mái?; leave me
alone (*don't bother me*) yàh mah
yôong gùp pŏm (chún)

already ... láir-o; I've already eaten
pŏm (chún) gin kâo láir-o

also ... dôo-ay; we also went to Hua
Hin rao bpai hŏo-a hĭn dôo-ay

alteration gahn bplèe-un bplairng

alternative: is there an alternative?
mee tahng lêu-uk mái?; we had no
alternative rao mâi mee tahng lêu-
uk

alternator orl-ter-nay-dtêr

although máir wâh

altogether túng mòt; what does that
come to altogether? túng mòt tâo-
rài?

always sa-mĕr

am *see page 98*

a.m.: at 3 a.m. dtee săhm; at 8 a.m.
sŏrng mohng cháo; *see page 111*

amazing mâi nâh chêu-a

ambassador àyk-ùk-ka-râht-cha-tôot

ambulance rót pa-yah-bahn; get an
ambulance rêe-uk rót pa-yah-bahn

America a-may-ri-gah

American (*adjective*) a-may-ri-gun; an
American/the Americans kon a-
may-ri-gun; I am American pŏm
(chún) bpen kon a-may-ri-gun

American plan gin yòo prórm

among nai ra-wàhng

amp: 13 amp fuse few sìp-săhm airm

amphoe (*subdivision of province*) um-
per

an(a)esthetic yah sa-lòp

ancestor bun-pa-bOo-ròot

anchor sa-mŏr

ancient boh-rahn; Ancient City

meu-ung boh-rahn; **in ancient times** sa-măi boh-rahn

and láir

angina rôhk sên loh-hìt dtèep

angry gròht; **I'm very angry about it** rêu-ung née pŏm (chún) gròht mâhk

animal sùt

ankle kôr táo

anniversary: it's our wedding anniversary today wun-née bpen wun króp rôrp dtàirng-ngahn kŏrng rao

annoy: he's annoying me káo tum hâi pŏm (chún) rum-kahn; **it's so annoying** nâh rum-kahn

anorak sêu-a kloom

another (*further*) èek; **another bottle, please** kŏr èek kòo-ut nèung krúp (kâ); **can we have another room?** (*a different one*) kŏr bplèe-un hôrng nòy dâi mái?

answer: there was no answer (*letter, conversation*) mâi mee kum dtòrp; (*telephone*) mâi mee kon rúp; **what was his answer?** káo dtòrp wâh yung-ngai?

ant: ants mót

antibiotics bpùti-chee-wa-ná

anticlimax mái sŏm wŭng

antihistamine yah airn-dtêe hít-dta-meen

antique boh-rahn wút-thòo; **is it a genuine antique?** bpen kŏrng gào táir táir rĕu bplào?

antique shop ráhn kăi kŏrng gào

any: have you got any coffee? mee gah-fair mái?; **I haven't got any** pŏm (chún) mâi mee

anybody (*at all*) krai gôr dâi; **can anybody help?** krai chôo-ay dâi bâhng?; **there wasn't anybody there** mâi mee krai yòo têe nûn; **who shall I ask?** — **anybody** ja tăhm krai? — krai gôr dâi

anything (*at all*) a-rai gôr dâi; **I don't want anything** pŏm (chún) mâi dtôrng-gahn a-rai; **don't you have anything else?** koon mâi mee a-rai

èek rĕu?; **what would you like to eat?** — **anything** ja gin a-rai? — a-rai gôr dâi

apart from nôrk jàhk

apartment a-páht-mén

apologize kŏr-tôht; **I do apologize** kŏr-tôht dôo-ay ná krúp (kâ)

appalling yâir

appear: it would appear that ... bprah-gòt wâh ...

appendicitis rôhk sâi dtìng

appetite: to have an appetite hĕw; **I've lost my appetite** pŏm (chún) mâi hĕw

apple aír-bpêrn

apple pie pai aír-bpêrn

application form bai sa-mùk

appointment: to make an appointment nút; **I'd like to make an appointment** pŏm (chún) kŏr nút

appreciate: thank you, I appreciate it kòrp-koon mâhk

approve: she doesn't approve káo mâi hĕn chôrp dôo-ay

April may-săh-yon

aqualung tŭng ah-gàht gùp nâh gàhk gun náhm

arch(a)eology boh-rahn-ka-dee

are *see page 98*

area: I don't know this (that) area pŏm (chún) mâi róo-jùk tăir-o née (nún)

area code ra-hùt

arm kăirn

around *see* **about**

arrangement: will you make the arrangements? koon jùt gahn hâi pŏm (chún) nòy dâi mái?

arrest jùp; **he's been arrested** káo tòok jùp

arrival kăh kâo

arrive mah tĕung; **when do we arrive?** rao ja tĕung mêu-a rài?; **has my parcel arrived yet?** hòr kŏrng pŏm (chún) mah tĕung láir-o rĕu yung?; **please let me know as soon as they arrive** mah tĕung láir-o, chôo-ay bòrk hâi sâhp dôo-ay; **we only arrived yesterday** rao pêrng

mah tĕung mêu-a wahn née
art sĭn-la-bpà
art gallery ráhn kăi pâhp kĕe-un
arthritis rôhk kôr ùk-sàyp
artificial tee-um
artist sĭn-la-bpin
as: as fast as you can ray-o tâo têe ja ray-o dâi; **as much as you can** mâhk tâo têe ja mâhk dâi; **as you like** dtahm jai koon; **as it's getting late** dèuk láir-o
ashore: to go ashore kêun fùng
ashtray têe kèe-a boo-rèe
aside from nôrk-jàhk
ask (*a question*) tăhm; (*for something*) kŏr; **that's not what I asked for** nûn mâi châi têe pŏm (chún) dtôrng-gahn; **could you ask him to phone me back?** koon chôo-ay bòrk hâi káo toh glùp mah hăa pŏm (chún) dâi mái?
asleep: he's still asleep káo yung norn lùp yòo
asparagus nòr-mái fa-rùng
aspirin air-sa-bprin
assault: she's been assaulted káo tòok tum rái; **she has been indecently assaulted** káo tòok chum-rao
assistant (*helper*) pôo-chôo-ay; (*in shop*) pa-núk ngahn kăi kŏrng
assume: I assume that ... pŏm (chún) kâo jai wâh ...
asthma rôhk hèut
astonishing nâh bpra-làht jai
astrologer mŏr-doo
astrology hŏh-rah-sàht
at: at the coffee shop têe kórp-fêe chórp; **at the hotel** têe rohng-rairm; **at 8 p.m.** way-lah sŏrng tôom; **see you at dinner** póp gun dtorn ah-

hăhn yen
atmosphere bun-yah-gàht
attractive sŏo-ay; **you're very attractive** koon sŏo-ay mâhk
aubergine ma-kĕu-a
auction gahn kăi lay-lŭng
audience (*listeners*) pôo-fung; (*viewers*) kon-doo
August sĭng-hăh-kom
aunt (*elder sister of mother or father*) bpâh; (*younger sister of father*) ah; (*younger sister of mother*) náh
Australia órt-sa-tray-lee-a
Australian (*adjective*) órt-sa-tray-lee-a; **an Australian/the Australians** kon órt-sa-tray-lee-a; **I am Australian** pŏm (chún) bpen kon órt-sa-tray-lee-a
authorities jâo-nâh-têe
automatic ùt-ta-noh-mút
automobile rót yon
autumn réu-doo bai-mái rôo-ung; **in the autumn** dtorn réu-doo bai-mái rôo-ung
available: when will it be available? ja mee mah mêu-a rài?; **when will he be available?** káo wâhng mêu-a rài?
average: the average Thai kon tai tôo-a tôo-a bpai; **an above average hotel** rohng-rairm dee dee nòy; **a below average hotel** rohng-rairm têe mâi kôy dee; **the food was only average** ah-hăhn tum-ma-dah tum-ma-dah; **on average** doy-ee cha-lèe-a
awake: is she awake? káo dtèun láir-o rĕu yung?
away: is it far away? yòo glai mái?; **go away!** bpái!
awful yâir mâhk
axle plao

B

baby dèk òrn
baby-carrier bplay hêw dèk
baby-sitter kon fâo dèk; **can you get us a baby-sitter?** hăh kon fâo dèk hâi rao kon nèung dâi mái?
bachelor chai sòht
back: I've got a bad back lŭng mây dee; **at the back** kâhng lŭng; **the back seat of the car** têe nûng kâhng lŭng; **I'll be right back** dĕe-o glùp mah; **when do you want it back?** ja ao keun mêu-a rài?; **can I have my money back?** kŏr ngern keun dâi mái?; **come back!** glùp mah nêe sée!; **I go back home tomorrow** prôong née pŏm (chún) ja glùp bâhn; **we'll be back next year** bpee nâh rao ja glùp mah èek; **when is the last bus back?** rót-may glùp têe-o sòot tái gèe mohng?
backache: I have a backache pŏm (chún) bpòo-ut lŭng
back door bpra-dtoo lŭng
backgammon bairk-gairm-morn
backpack gra-bpăo kwâi lŭng
back seat têe nûng kâhng lŭng
back street ta-nŏn kâhng nai
bacon mŏo bay-korn; **bacon and eggs** mŏo bay-korn gùp kài dao
bad mâi dee; **this meat's bad** néu-a sĕe-a láir-o; **a bad headache** bpòo-ut hŏo-a mâhk; **it's not bad** mâi lay-o; **too bad!** (*ironic*) yâir jung!
badly: he's badly injured káo bàht jèp săh-hùt
bag (*paper bag, carrier bag*) tŏong; (*suitcase, briefcase, handbag*) gra-bpăo
baggage gra-bpăo dern tahng
baggage allowance (*weight*) núm nùk gra-bpăo

baggage checkroom têe fàhk gra-bpăo
baht (*unit of currency*) bàht
bakery ráhn tum ka-nŏm-bpung
balcony ra-bee-ung; **a room with a balcony** hôrng mee ra-bee-ung; **on the balcony** bon ra-bee-ung
bald hŏo-a láhn
ball lôok born
ball-point pen bpàhk-gah lôok lêun
bamboo mái pài
bamboo shoot(s) nòr mái
banana glôo-ay
band (*music*) wong don-dtree
bandage pâh pun plăir; **could you change the bandage?** chôo-ay bplèe-un pâh pun plăir hâi nòy dâi mái?
bandaid bplah-sa-dter
bandit john
Bangkok groong-tâyp
bank (*money*) ta-nah-kahn; **when are the banks open?** ta-nah-kahn bpèrt gèe mohng?
bank (*of river*) fùng
bank account bun-chee ngern fàhk ta-nah-kahn
bar bah
barber(shop) ráhn dtùt pŏm
bargain (*haggle over price*) dtòr rah-kah; **it's a real bargain** tòok dee
barrette kĕm nèep pŏm
bartender bah ten-dêr
basic: the hotel is rather basic rohng rairm tum-ma-dah; **will you teach me some basic phrases?** chôo-ay sŏrn kum têe jum-bpen hâi nòy dâi mái?
basket dta-grâh
bath, bathtub àhng àhp náhm; **can I take a bath?** kŏr àhp náhm dâi mái?

bathing costume chóot àhp náhm
bathrobe sêu-a kloom
bathroom hôrng náhm; **a room with
a private bathroom** hôrng norn têe
mee hôrng náhm dôo-ay; **can I use
your bathroom?** kǒr chái hôrng
náhm nòy dâi mái?
bath towel pâh chét dtoo-a
battery bair-dta-rêe; **the battery's flat**
bair-dta-rêe mòt
bay ào
bazaar bah-sah
be bpen; **don't be lazy** yàh kêe gèe-
ut; **where have you been?** bpai nǎi
mah?; **I've never been to Phuket**
pǒm (chún) mâi ker-ee bpai poo-gèt;
see page 98
beach chai-hàht; **on the beach** têe
chai-hàht; **I'm going to the beach**
pǒm (chún) bpai chai-hàht
beach hut gra-tôrm chai ta-lay
beach mat sèu-a bpoo chai-hàht
beach towel pâh chét dtoo-a sǔm-rùp
chai-hàht
beach umbrella rôm gun dàirt
beads lôok bpùt
beans tòo-a
beard krao
beautiful (*in appearance*) sǒo-ay; (*in
sound*) prór; **thank you, that's
beautiful** kòrp-koon mâhk, sǒo-ay
dee
beauty salon ráhn sěrm sǒo-ay
because prór; **because of the weather**
prór ah-gàht
bed dtee-ung; **single bed** dtee-ung
dèe-o; **double bed** dtee-ung kôo; **my
bed hasn't been made** yung mâi dâi
tum têe-norn; **he's still in bed** káo
yung norn yòo; **I'm going to bed**
pǒm (chún) bpai norn
bed linen pâh bpoo têe-norn
bedroom hôrng norn
bee pêung
beef néu-a woo-a
beer bee-a; **two beers, please** kǒr
bee-a sǒrng kòo-ut
before gòrn; **before breakfast** gòrn
ah-hǎhn cháo; **before I leave** gòrn

bpai; **I haven't been here before**
pǒm (chún) mâi ker-ee mah têe nêe
(mah gòrn)
beggar kǒr-tahn
begin rêrm; **when does it begin?**
rêrm mêu-a rài?
beginner: I'm just a beginner pǒm
(chún) pêrng rêrm ree-un
beginning: at the beginning dtorn
dtôn
behavio(u)r kwahm bpra-préut
behind kâhng lǔng; **the driver
behind me** kon kùp kâhng lǔng
beige sěe néu-a
believe: I don't believe you/it pǒm
(chún) mâi chêu-a; **I believe you**
pǒm (chún) chêu-a
bell (*large, e.g. temple bell*) ra-kung;
(*small*) gra-ding; (*electrical*) grìng
belong: that belongs to me nûn
kǒrng pǒm (chún); **who does this
belong to?** nêe kǒrng krai?
belongings: all my belongings kâo
kǒrng kǒrng pǒm (chún) túng mòt
below dtâi; **below the knee** dtâi hǒo-a
kào
belt (*clothing*) kěm kùt
bend (*in road*) hǒo-a kóhng
berth têe-norn
beside: beside the temple kâhng
kâhng wút; **sit beside me** nûng
kâhng pǒm (chún)
besides: besides that nôrk jàhk nún
best dee têe sòot; **the best hotel in
town** rohng rairm dee têe sòot nai
meu-ung née; **that's the best meal
I've ever had** bpen ah-hǎhn têe a-
ròy têe sòot têe ker-ee tahn mah
bet: I bet you 500 baht pǒm (chún)
táh pa-nun hâh róy bàht
better dee gwàh; **it's better** dee gwàh;
**going by taxi is better than going
by bus** bpai táirk-sêe dee gwàh bpai
rót-may; **this one is better** nêe dee
gwàh; **it's better than mine** dee
gwàh kǒrng pǒm (chún); **which one
is better?** un nǎi dee gwàh?; **to get
better** dee kêun; **that's better!** dee
kêun láir-o; **are you feeling better?**

kôy yung chôo-a mái?; **I'm feeling a
lot better** pǒm (chún) kôy yung
chôo-a; **I'd better be going now**
pǒm (chún) dtôrng bpai láir-o
between ra-wàhng
beyond ler-ee bpai; **beyond the
mountains** ler-ee poo-kǎo bpai
bicycle jùk-gra-yahn; **can we rent
bicycles here?** têe nêe mee jùk-gra-
yahn hâi châo mái?
big yài; **a big one** un yài; **that's too
big** yài gern bpai; **it's not big
enough** yài mâi por
bigger yài gwàh
bike jùk-gra-yahn
bikini bi-gi-nee
bill bin; **could I have the bill,
please?** kǒr bin krúp (kâ), gèp
ngern krúp (kâ)
billfold gra-bpǎo sa-dtung
billiards bin-lêe-ut
bird nók
biro (tm) bpàhk-gah lôok lêun
birthday wun gèrt; **it's my birthday**
bpen wun gèrt pǒm (chún); **when is
your birthday?** wun gèrt koon
mêu-a rài?; **happy birthday!** sòok
sǔn wun gèrt
biscuit kóo-gêe
bit: just a little bit for me pee-ung
nít dee-o tâo-nún; **a big bit** chín yài;
a bit of that cake káyk nûn chín
nèung; **it's a bit too big** mun yài
bpai nòy; **it's a bit too much for me
thanks** mun mâhk bpai nòy krúp
(kâ); **it's a bit cold today** wun née
ah-gàht yen bpai nòy
bite gùt; **I've been bitten (by a ...)**
pǒm (chún) tòok ... gùt; **do you
have something for bites?** mee yah
gâir kun mái?
bitter (taste) kǒm
black dum; **black and white film**
feem kǎo dum
blackout: he's had a blackout káo
nâh mêut
bladder gra-pór bpù-sǎh-wá
blanket pâh hòm; **I'd like another
blanket** kǒr pâh hòm èek pěun

nèung krúp (kâ)
bleach (for toilet etc) yah láhng hôrng
náhm
bleed lêu-ut òrk; **he's bleeding** káo
lêu-ut òrk
bless you! the Thais have no phrase said
to someone who sneezes
blind dtah bòrt
blinds môo-lêe
blister plǎir porng
blocked (road, drain) dtun
block of flats dtèuk
blond (adjective) pǒm sěe torng
blonde pôo-yǐng pǒm sěe torng
blood lêu-ut; **his blood group is ...**
lêu-ut glòom káo keu ...; **I have
high blood pressure** pǒm (chún)
mee kwahm dun loh-hìt sǒong
blouse sêu-a pôo-yǐng
blue sěe núm ngern; **light blue** sěe
fáh
board: full-board gin yòo prórm;
half-board mâi roo-um ah-hǎhn
glahng wun
boarding pass bùt têe-nûng
boat reu-a
body râhng gai
boil (on body) fěe; **boil the water** dtôm
náhm
boiled egg kài dtôm
boiled rice kâo sǒo-ay
boiling hot (weather, food) rórn mâhk
bomb (noun) lôok ra-bèrt
bone (in meat, body, fish) gra-dòok
bonnet (of car) gra-bprohng rót
book (noun) núng-sěu; (verb) jorng;
I'd like to book a table for two kǒr
jorng dtó sǒrng têe
bookshop, bookstore ráhn kǎi núng-
sěu
boot (on foot) rorng-táo; (of car) gra-
bprohng tái rót
booze lâo; **I had too much booze**
pǒm (chún) gin lâo mâhk gern bpai
border (of country) chai dairn
bored: I'm bored pǒm (chún) bèu-a
boring (person, trip, film) nâh bèu-a
born: I was born in ... (place) pǒm
(chún) gèrt têe ...; **I was born on ...**

(*date*) pŏm (chún) gèrt wun têe ...
borrow: may I borrow ...? kŏr yeum ... dâi mái?
boss jâo nai
both túng sŏrng; **I'll take both of them** pŏm (chún) ao túng sŏrng; **we'll both come** rao bpai túng sŏrng kon
bother: sorry to bother you kŏr-tôht têe róp-goo-un; **it's no bother** mâi yôong a-rai ròrk; **it's such a bother** yôong jing jing
bottle kòo-ut; **a bottle of wine** wai kòo-ut nèung; **another bottle, please** kŏr èek kòo-ut nèung
bottle-opener têe bpèrt kòo-ut
bottom (*body*) gôn; **at the bottom of the hill** dteen kăo; **at the bottom of the soi** (*lane*) sòot soy
bottom gear gee-a nèung
bowels tórng
bowl chahm; **a bowl of noodles** góo-ay dtĕe-o chahm nèung
bowling boh-lîng
box hèep
boxer núk moo-ay
boxing (*international*) moo-ay (săh-gon); (*Thai style*) moo-ay tai
boxing stadium sa-năhm moo-ay
box office hôrng kăi dtŏo-a
boy dèk chai
boyfriend: my boyfriend fairn chún
bra sêu-a yók song
bracelet gum-lai meu
brake fluid núm mun bràyk
brake lining pâh dàht hâhm lór
brakes bràyk; **there's something wrong with the brakes** bràyk sĕe-a; **can you check the brakes?** chôo-ay chék-doo bràyk nòy, dâi mái?; **I had to brake suddenly** pŏm (chún) dtôrng yèe-up bràyk tun-tee
branch (*of tree*) gìng mái; (*of bank*) săh-kăh
brand dtrah, yêe hôr
brandy lâo brùn-dee
brave (*daring*) glâh hăhn; (*in accepting adversity*) gùt fun ton
bread ka-nŏm-bpung; **is there any**

bread and butter? mee ka-nŏm-bpung gùp ner-ee sòt mái?; **some more bread, please** kŏr ka-nŏm-bpung èek krúp (kâ)
break (*verb*) hùk, dtàirk; **I think I've broken my ankle** pŏm (chún) kít wâh kôr táo hùk; **it keeps breaking** mun hùk/dtàirk yòo rêu-ay
breakdown: I've had a breakdown (*car*) rót pŏm (chún) sĕe-a; **nervous breakdown** bpra-sàht sĕe-a
breakfast ah-hăhn cháo
break in: somebody's broken in mee ka-moy-ee kâo bâhn
breast nom
breast-fed gin nom mâir
breath lom hăi jai; **out of breath** hăi jai mâi tun
breathe hăi jai; **I can't breathe** pŏm (chún) hăi jai mâi òrk
breathtaking: breathtakingly beautiful sŏo-ay yàhng bòrk mâi tòok
breeze lom òrn òrn
breezy mee lom òrn òrn
bride jâo-săo
bridegroom jâo-bào
bridge (*over river*) sa-pahn
brief (*stay, visit*) sûn sûn
briefcase gra-bpăo
bright (*light*) sa-wàhng; (*colour*) jùt
brilliant (*idea*) yêe-um; (*colour*) jùt
bring (*something*) ao ... mah; (*someone*) pah ... mah; **could you bring my baggage to the hotel?** ao gra-bpăo pŏm (chún) mah têe rohng rairm dâi mái?; **I'll bring the newspaper back** pŏm (chún) ja ao núng-sĕu-pim mah keun; **can I bring a friend too?** pah pêu-un mah dôo-ay dâi mái?
Britain bpra-tâyt ung-grìt
British (*adjective*) ung-grìt; **the British** kon ung-grìt; **I'm British** pŏm (chún) bpen kon ung-grìt
Briton kon ung-grìt
broke: I'm broke pŏm (chún) tŭng dtàirk
broken dtàirk láir-o; (*out of order*) sĕe-a; **you've broken it** koon tum dtàirk; **it's broken** mun dtàirk láir-o;

(*out of order*) sĕe-a láir-o; **broken nose** ja-mòok hùk

bronze loh-hà sŭm-rít

brooch kĕm glùt sêu-a

brother: older brother pêe chai; **younger brother** nórng chai; **my older/younger brother** pêe/nórng chai kŏrng pŏm (chún)

brother-in-law: older brother-in-law pêe kĕr-ee; **younger brother-in-law** nórng kĕr-ee

brown sĕe núm dtahn; **I don't go brown** pŏm mâi klúm

browse: may I just browse around? kŏr chom gòrn dâi mái?

bruise (*noun*) fók-chúm

brunette pôo-yĭng pŏm sĕe núm dtahn

brush (*noun*) mái gwàht

bubble bath núm yah àhp náhm

bucket tŭng

Buddha prá-póot-ta-jâo; **Buddha image** prá-póot-ta-rôop

Buddhism sàht-sa-năh póot

Buddhist: he is a Buddhist káo núp tĕu sàht-sa-năh póot; **Buddhist holy day** wun prá

buffet bòop-fay

bug (*insect*) ma-lairng; **she's caught a stomach bug** káo tórng sĕe-a

building ah-kahn

bulb (*electrical*) lòrt fai fáh; **a new bulb** lòrt fai fáh mài

bull woo-a dtoo-a pôo

bump (*verb*) chon; **I bumped my head** hŏo-a chon

bumper (*of car*) gun chon

bumpy (*road*) ta-nŏn kròo krà; (*flight*) mâi rêe-up

bunch of flowers chôr dòrk-mái

bungalow bung-gah-loh

bunion dtah bplah

bunk beds dtee-ung sŏrng chún

buoy tôon

burglar ka-moy-ee

Burma bpra-tâyt pa-mâh

Burmese (*adjective*) pa-mâh; **a Burmese/the Burmese** kon pa-mâh

burn: do you have an ointment for

burns? mee yah tah sŭm-rùp néu-a mâi mái?

burnt: this meat is burnt néu-a mâi; **my arms are so burnt** kăirn pŏm (chún) mâi dàirt

burst: a burst pipe tôr dtàirk

bus rót may; **air-conditioned bus** rót may bprùp ah-gàht; **tour bus** (*inter-province*) rót too-a; **number 16 bus** rót may săi sìp hòk; **is this the bus for ...?** rót may săi née bpai ... châi mái?; **when's the next bus?** rót kun nâh òrk gèe mohng?; **what time does the bus to Nakhorn Phanom leave?** rót may bpai na-korn pa-nom òrk gèe mohng?

bus driver kon kùp rót may

business tóo-rá; **I'm here on business** pŏm (chún) mah tóo-rá têe-nêe; **it's a pleasure to do business with you** yin dee têe dâi tum tóo-ra-gìt gùp koon; **it's none of your business** mâi châi tóo-rá kŏrng koon

businessman núk tóo-rá-gìt

bus station, bus terminal sa-tăhn-ee rót may

bus stop bpâi rót may; **will you tell me which bus stop I get off at?** chôo-ay bòrk pŏm wâh dtôrng long rót may têe năy

bust (*of body*) nâh òk

bus tour too-a

busy (*street*) jor-jair; (*restaurant*) nâirn; **I'm busy this evening** keun-née pŏm (chún) mâi wâhng; **the line was busy** (*telephone*) săi mâi wâhng

but dtàir; **not ... but ...** mâi châi ... dtàir bpen ...

butcher ráhn néu-a

butter ner-ee sòt

butterfly pĕe sĕu-a

button gra-doom

buy séu; **I'd like to buy ...** pŏm (chún) yàhk séu ...; **where can I buy ...?** pŏm (chún) séu ... dâi têe năi?

by: by train/car/boat doy-ee rót fai/rót yon/reu-a; **who's it written by?** krai bpen kon dtàirng?; **I came by**

myself pǒm (chún) mah ayng; **a seat
by the window** têe nûng dtìt nâh
dtàhng; **by the sea** chai ta-lay; **can
you do it by Wednesday?** koon ja
tum hâi sèt gòrn wun póot dâi mái?
bye-bye lah gòrn

C

cab (*taxi*) táirk-sêe
cabaret kah-bah-ray
cabbage ga-lùm-bplee
cable (*electrical*) sǎi kay-bern
café ráhn gǒo-ay dtěe-o
caffeine kah-feen
cake ka-nǒm káyk; **a piece of cake**
ka-nǒm káyk chín nèung
calculator krêu-ung kít lâyk
calendar bpà-dti-tin
call: to call, to be called rêe-uk; **what
is this called?** nêe rêe-uk wâh a-
rai?; **call the manager!** rêe-uk pôo-
jùt-gahn see!; **to make a telephone
call** toh-ra-sùp, toh; **I'd like to make
a call to England** pǒm (chún) yàhk
ja toh-ra-sùp bpai bpra-tâyt ung-grìt;
I'll call back later (*come back*) pǒm
(chún) ja glùp mah tee lǔng; (*phone
back*) pǒm (chún) ja toh glùp mah
tee lǔng; **I'm expecting a call from
London** pǒm kôy toh-ra-sùp jàhk
lorn-dorn; **would you give me a call
at 7.30?** chôo-ay toh mah dtorn
tôom krêung ná; **it's been called off**
ngót bpai láir-o
call box dtôo-toh-ra-sùp
calm (*person*) kon jai yen; (*sea*) sa-
ngòp; **calm down!** jai yen yen ná!
calories kair-lor-rêe
Cambodia bpra-tâyt gum-poo-chaa
Cambodian (*adjective*) ka-mǎyn; **a
Cambodian/the Cambodians** kon
ka-mǎyn
camera glôrng tài rôop
can (*tin*) gra-bpǒrng; **canned milk**
nom gra-bpǒrng

can (*may, might*) dâi; (*be capable of*)
bpen; **can I ...?** pǒm (chún) ... dâi
mái?; **can you ...?** koon ... dâi mái?;
can you help me? koon chôo-ay
pǒm (chún) dâi mái?; **can he/she ...?**
káo ... dâi mái?; **can we ...?** rao ...
dâi mái?; **can they ...?** káo ... dâi
mái?; **I can't ...** pǒm (chún) ... mâi
dâi; **he can't ...** káo ... mâi dâi; **can
I keep it?** pǒm (chún) gèp wái dâi
mái?; **I can't speak Thai** pǒm (chún)
pôot pah-sǎh tai mâi bpen; **can you
drive?** koon kùp rót bpen mái?; **that
can't be right** mun kong mâi tòok
Canada bpra-tâyt kair-nah-dah
Canadian (*adjective*) kair-nah-dah; **a
Canadian/the Canadians** kon kair-
nah-dah; **I'm Canadian** pǒm (chún)
bpen kon kair-nah-dah
canal klorng
cancel ngót; **can I cancel my reservation?** pǒm kǒr ngót gahn sǔng
jorng wái; **can we cancel dinner for
tonight?** keun née ngót ah-hǎhn
yen, dâi mái?; **I cancelled it** pǒm
(chún) sǔng ngót
cancellation gahn sǔng ngót
candle tee-un
candies lôok gwàht; **a piece of candy**
lôok gwàht un nèung
can-opener têe bpèrt gra-bpǒrng
cap moo-ùk; **bathing cap** moo-ùk àhp
náhm
capital city meu-ung lǒo-ung
capital letters dtoo-a yài
capsize: it capsized kwûm
captain (*of ship*) gùp-dtun

car rót, rót-yon
carat: is it 9(14) carat gold? bpen torng gâo (sìp sèe) gah-rùt rěu bplào?
carbonated núm ma-nét
carburet(t)or kah-ber-ret-dtêr
card: do you have a (business) card? mee nahm bùt mái?
cardboard box glòrng gra-dàht kǎirng
cardigan sêu-a nǎo
cards pâi; do you play cards? lên pâi bpen mái?
care: to take care of doo-lair; will you take care of this bag for me? chôo-ay doo-lair gra-bpǎo née nòy, dâi mái?; care of ... pàhn ...
careful: be careful ra-wung!
careless: that was careless of you koon nêe múk ngâi ná; careless driving kùp rót bpra-màht
car hire bor-ri-gahn rót châo; do you have any cars for hire? mee rót hâi châo mái?
car keys goon-jair rót
carnival ngahn
car park têe jòrt rót
carpet prom
car rental (place) sa-tǎhn bor-ri-gahn rót châo
carry (something in the hands) těu; (something by a handle) hêw; (a heavy load on the back or shoulder) bàirk; (a child, in one's arms) ôom; could you carry this for me? chôo-ay hêw hâi nòy dâi máy?
carry-all gra-bpǎo
carry-cot dta-grâh sài dèk
car-sick mao rót; I get car-sick easily pǒm (chún) mao rót ngâi
carton glòrng; a carton of milk glòrng nom
carving rôop gàir sa-lùk
carwash bor-ri-gahn láhng rót
case (suitcase) gra-bpǎo; in any case nôrk jàhk nún; in that case tâh yung ngún; it's a special case bpen gor-ra-nee pi-sàyt; in case he comes back pèu-a káo glùp mah; I'll take

two just in case ao pèu-a wái sǒrng un
cash ngern sòt; I don't have any cash pǒm (chún) mâi mee ngern sòt; I'll pay cash pǒm (chún) jài bpen ngern sòt; will you cash a cheque/check for me? kǒr kêun ngern nòy
cashdesk dtó jài ngern
cash dispenser bor-ri-gahn ngern dòo-un
cash register krêu-ung kít ngern
casino kah-si-noh
cassette móo-un tâyp kah-set
cassette player, cassette recorder krêu-ung lên tâyp kah-set
castle bpra-sàht
casual: casual clothes sêu-a pâh dtahm sa-bai
cat mair-o
catastrophe kwahm hǎi-ya-ná
catch (ball, thief) jùp; to catch a bus kêun rót may; where do we catch the bus? rao kêun rót may têe nǎi?; he's caught some strange illness káo dùt rôhk bpra-làht
catching: is it catching? (disease) bpen rôhk dtìt dtòr rěu bplào?
Catholic kah-tor-lík, krít-dtung
Caucasian fa-rùng
cauliflower dòrk ga-lùm-bplee
cause (noun) hàyt; (verb) tum hâi
cave tûm
ceiling pay-dahn
celebrations ngahn cha-lǒrng
cellophane gra-dàht gâir-o
cemetery bpàh cháh
center jai glahng; see also centre
centigrade sen-dti-gràyd; see page 115
centimetre, centimeter sen-dti-mét; see page 113
central glahng meu-ung; we'd prefer something more central rao chôrp glahng meu-ung mâhk gwàh
central hospital rohng pa-yah-bahn glahng
central post office bprai-sa-nee glahng
central region (of Thailand) pâhk

glahng
centre (*of town*) jai glahng; **how do we get to the centre?** bpai jai glahng meu-ung yung-ngai?; **in the centre (of town)** yòo jai glahng meu-ung; **shopping centre** sŏon gahn káh
century sa-ta-wút; **in the 19th/20th century** sa-ta-wút têe sìp gâo/yêe sìp
ceramics krêu-ung bpûn din pǎo
certain nâir jai; **are you certain?** nâir jai rěu?; **I'm absolutely certain** pǒm (chún) nâir jai yàhng têe sòot
certainly nâir-norn; **certainly not!** mâi ròrk!
certificate: certificate of guarantee bai rúp rorng; **birth certificate** bai sòot-ti-bùt; **marriage certificate** bai ta-bee-un sǒm-rót
chain (*for bike, padlocks etc*) sôh; (*around neck*) sôy kor
chair gâo-êe
chambermaid yǐng rúp chái
champagne chairm-payn
chance (*opportunity*) oh-gàht; **quite by chance** bung-ern; **no chance!** mâi mee tahng!
change: could you change this into baht coins? kǒr lâirk bpen rěe-un bàht dâi mái?; **I haven't got any change** pǒm (chún) mâi mee báirnk yôy yôy; **can you give me change for 100 baht?** kǒr dtàirk bai la róy nòy, dâi mái?; **do we have to change (trains)?** dtôrng bplèe-un rót fai rěu bplào?; **for a change** bplèe-un bun-yah-gàht; **the sheets haven't been changed** yung mâi dâi bplèe-un pâh bpoo; **it has changed so much** bplée-un bpai mâhk; **do you want to change places with me?** bplée-un têe gun, ao mái?; **can I change this for ...?** kǒr lâirk âi nêe bpen ... dâi mái?
changeable (*weather*) bplèe-un bplairng
changwat (*province*) jung-wùt
chaos sùp sǒn on-la-màhn
chap kon nún; **the chap at reception** kon nún têe pa-nàirk dtôrn rúp

charge: is there an extra charge? mee gahn kít ngern èek dtàhng hàhk mái?; **what do you charge?** kít rah-kah tâo-rài?; **who's in charge here?** têe nêe krai bpen hǒo-a nâh?
charming mee sa-nàsy
chart (*for navigation*) pǎirn têe; (*diagram*) pǎirn pǔng
charter flight têe-o bin mǎo
chassis krohng rót
chat (*verb*) koo-ee
cheap tòok; **do you have something cheaper?** mee a-rai tòok gwàh rěu bplào?
cheat: I've been cheated pǒm (chún) tòok gohng
check: will you check first? chôo-ay chék doo gòrn dâi mái?; **will you check the steering?** chôo-ay dtròo-ut poo-ung mah-lai nòy; **will you check the bill?** chôo-ay chék doo bin nòy; **I've checked it** pǒm (chún) chék doo láir-o
check (*for money*) chék; **will you take a check?** jài bpen chék, dâi mái?
check (*bill*) bin; **may I have the check please?** kǒr bin nòy
checkbook sa-mòot chék
checked (*shirt*) lai dtah màhk róok
checkers dtah màhk róok
check-in dtròo-ut chûng núm-nùk
checkroom (*for coats etc*) têe fàhk kǒrng
cheek (*on face*) gâirm; **what a cheek!** lèe-um sǒong jung!
cheeky (*person*) lèe-um sǒong
cheerio (*bye-bye*) bai bai ná
cheers (*toast*) *the Thais don't say anything when starting to drink*
cheer up yím nòy nâh
cheese ner-ee kǎirng
chef hǒo-a nâh kon tum kroo-a
chemist (*shop*) ráhn kǎi yah
cheque chék; **will you take a cheque?** jai bpen chék, dâi mái?
cheque book sa-mòot chék
cheque card bùt chék
cherry chair-rêe
chess màhk róok

chest (*body*) nâh-òk
chewing gum màhk fa-rùng
Chiangmai chee-ung mài
chicken gài; **barbecued chicken** gài yâhng; **chicken curry** gairng gài
chicken fried rice kâo pùt gài
chickenpox ee-sòok ee-săi
child, children dèk; (*one's own*) lôok; **Thai children** dèk tai; **our children** lôok kŏrng rao
child minder kon lée-ung doo dèk
child minding service bor-ri-gahn lée-ung doo dèk
children's playground sa-năhm dèk lên
children's pool sà wâi náhm dèk
children's room hôrng dèk
chilled (*wine, beer, bottled drinks*) yen jùt; **it's not properly chilled** kòo-ut née mâi yen jùt
chilli prík
chilli sauce núm prík
chilly yen
chimney bplòrng fai
chin kahng
china jahn gra-bêu-ung
China bpra-tâyt jeen
Chinese (*adjective*) jeen; (*language*) pah-săh jeen; **a Chinese/the Chinese** kon jeen; **Chinese food** ah-hăhn jeen; **Chinese restaurant** ráhn ah-hăhn jeen
chips mun fa-rùng tôrt; **potato chips** mun fa-rùng tôrt
chocolate chork-goh-lairt
choke (*on car*) chóhk
cholera à-hi-wah
choose: it's hard to choose lêu-uk yâhk; **you choose for us** chôo-ay lêu-uk hâi nòy
chopsticks dta-gèe-up
Christian: he is a Christian kao núp tĕu sàh-sa-năh krít
Christian name chêu
Christmas krít-sa-maht
church bòht; **where is the Protestant/Catholic church?** bòht krít-tee-un/kah-tor-lík yòo têe năi?
cigar si-gah

cigarette boo-rèe; **tipped cigarettes** boo-rèe gôn grorng
cigarette lighter fai cháirk
cine-camera glôrng tài nŭng
cinema rohng nŭng
circle (*shape*) wong glom
citizen: I'm a British/American citizen pŏm (chún) mee sŭn-châht ung-grìt/a-may-ri-gun
city meu-ung
city centre, city center jai glahng meu-ung
civil servant kâh-râht-cha-gahn
claim (*noun: insurance*) gahn rêe-uk kâh bpra-gun keun
claim form bàirp form rêe-uk ngern keun
clarify chée jairng
class: first class chún nèung; **second class** chún sŏrng; **third class** chún săhm
classical: Thai classical music dondtree tai derm
clean (*adjective*) sa-àht; **it's not clean** mâi sa-àht; **may I have some clean sheets?** kŏr pâh bpoo têe-norn mài mài; **our apartment hasn't been cleaned today** wun née hôrng yung mâi dâi tum kwahm sa-àht; **can you clean this for me?** tum kwahm sa-àht wái nêe hâi nòy dâi mái?
cleaning solution (*for contact lenses*) núm yah tum kwahm sa-àht
cleansing cream (*cosmetic*) kreem láhng nâh
clear: it's not very clear mâi kôy chút; **OK, that's clear** oh-kay, chút láir-o
clever cha-làht
cliff nâh păh
climate ah-gàht
climb (*verb*) bpèen
clinic klee-ník
cloakroom (*for coats, handbags etc*) têe fàhk kŏrng; (*WC*) hôrng náhm
clock nah-li-gah
close: to be close (*near*) glâi; **is it close?** yòo glâi mái?; **close to the hotel** glâi glâi rohng rairm; **close by**

yòo glâi glâi; (*weather*) òp âo
close (*shut*) bpìt; **when do you close?**
bpìt gèe mohng?
closed bpìt; **they were closed** bpìt
láir-o
closet (*toilet*) hôrng náhm; (*cupboard*)
dtôo
cloth (*material*) pâh; (*rag*) pâh kêe réw
clothes sêu-a pâh
clothes line rao dtàhk pâh
clothes peg, clothespin mái nèep
pâh
clouds mâyk; **it's clouding over** mee
mâyk fŏn
cloudy mâyk kréum
club, clubhouse sa-moh-sŏrn
clumsy sôom sâhm
clutch (*car*) klút; **the clutch is slip-ping** klút lêun
coach (*long distance bus*) rót too-a
coach trip rót num têe-o; **is there a coach trip to ...?** mee rót num têe-o
bpai ... mái?
coast chai ta-lay; **at the coast** chai ta-lay
coat (*overcoat etc*) sêu-a kloom; (*jacket*)
sêu-a nôrk
coathanger mái kwăirn sêu-a
cobbler châhng rorng táo
cobra ngoo hào
cockroach ma-lairng sàhp
cocktail kórk-tayn
cocktail bar hôrng kórk-tayn
cocoa goh-gôh
coconut ma-práo
coconut juice núm ma-práo
**code: what's the (dialling) code for
...?** ra-hùt ... ber a-rai?
coffee gah-fair; **a white coffee, a
coffee with milk** gah-fair sài nom;
a black coffee gah-fair dum; **two
coffees, please** kŏr gah-fair sŏrng
tôo-ay
coffee shop kòrp-fêe chórp
coin ngern rĕe-un
Coke (*tm*) koh-lâh
cold (*adjective*) yen; **to feel cold** năo;
I'm cold pŏm (chún) năo; **I have a
cold** pŏm (chún) bpen wùt

coldbox (*for carrying food*) glòrng núm
kăirng
cold cream (*cosmetic*) kreem sa-măhn
pĕw
collapse: he's collapsed (*lost conscious-ness*) káo mòt sa-dtì
collar (*of shirt*) kor bpòk sêu-a
collar bone gra-dòok hăi bplah-ráh
colleague (*at work*) pêu-un rôo-um
ngahn; **my colleague** pêu-un rôo-um ngahn kŏrng pŏm (chún); **your
colleague** pêu-un rôo-um ngahn
kŏrng koon
collect: I've come to collect ... pŏm
(chún) mah gèp ...; **I collect ...**
(*stamps etc*) pŏm (chún) sa-sŏm ...; **I
want to call New York collect** pŏm
(chún) ja toh gèp ngern bplai tahng
bpai new yórk
collect call toh gèp ngern bplai
tahng
college wít-ta-yah-lai
collide chon
collision: there's been a collision
(*cars*) mee rót chon gun
cologne núm hŏrm
colo(u)r sĕe; **do you have any other
colo(u)rs?** mee sĕe èun èek mái?
colo(u)r film feem sĕe
comb (*noun*) wĕe
come mah; **I come from London**
pŏm (chún) mah jàhk lorn-dorn;
where do you come from? koon
mah jàhk năi krúp (ká)?; **when are
they coming?** káo mah mêu-a rài?;
come here mah nêe; **come with me**
bpai gùp pŏm (chún); **come back!**
glùp mah nêe!; **I'll come back later**
dĕe-o ja glùp mah; **come in!** chern
kâo mah; **he's coming on very well**
(*improving*) káo kôy yung chôo-a;
come on! (*I don't believe you*) mây
chêu-a; (*hurry up*) ray-o ray-o nòy!;
do you want to come out this eve-ning? yen née yàhk bpai têe-o mái?;
these two pictures didn't come out
sŏrng rôop née tài sĕe-a; **the money
hasn't come through yet** ngern
yung mah mâi tĕung

comfortable (*hotel etc*) sa-dòo-uk sa-bai; **it's not very comfortable** mâi kôy sa-dòo-uk sa-bai

communist korm-mew-nít

company (*firm*) bor-ri-sùt

compare bprèe-up têe-up

comparison: **there's no comparison** bprèe-up (têe-up) gun mâi dâi

compartment (*train*) dtôo

compass kěm-tít

compensation kâh chót cher-ee

complain (*grumble*) bòn; (*make a complaint*) dtòr wâh; **I want to complain about my room** pǒm kǒr dtòr wâh rêu-ung hôrng nòy

complaint kôr glào hǎh; **I have a complaint** pǒm mee rêu-ung ja dtòr wâh

complete: **the complete set** króp chóot; **it's a complete disaster** mun yâir jing jing ler-ee

completely túng mòt

complicated: **it's very complicated** yôong yâhk mâhk

comprehensive (*insurance*) bpra-gun bèt sèt

compulsory pâhk bung-kúp

computer korm-pew-dtêr

concerned (*anxious*) bpen hòo-ung; **we are very concerned** rao bpen hòo-ung mâhk

concert gahn sa-dairng don-dtree

concussion sa-mǒrng tòok gra-tóp gra-teu-un

condenser (*in car*) korn-den-ser

condition: **it's not in very good condition** sa-pâhp mâi kôy dee

conditioner (*for hair*) kreem nôo-ut pǒm

condom tǒong yahng, bplòrk

conductor (*on train*) gaht; **bus conductor** gra-bpǎo rót may

conference gahn bpra-choom

confirm: **can you confirm the reservation?** chôo-ay korn-ferm têe jorng wái láir-o, dâi mái?

confuse: **it's very confusing** sùp sǒn mâhk

congratulations! kǒr sa-dairng kwahm yin dee

conjunctivitis rôhk yêu-a bòo dtah ùk-sàyp

connection (*in travelling*) dtòr

conscious (*medically*) mee sa-dtì

consciousness: **he's lost consciousness** káo sîn sa-dtì

constipation tórng pòok

consul gong-soon

consulate sa-tǎhn gong-sǒon

contact (*verb*) dtìt dtòr; **how can I contact ...?** pǒm (chún) dtìt dtòr gùp ... dâi yung-ngai?; **I'm trying to contact ...** pǒm (chún) pa-yah-yahm dtìt dtòr gùp ...

contact lenses korn-táirk layn

contraceptive (*noun*) krêu-ung koom gum-nèrt

convenient (*time, location*) sa-dòo-uk; **that's not convenient** nûn mâi̊ kôy sa-dòo-uk

cook: **it's not properly cooked** (*is underdone*) yung mâi sòok; **it's beautifully cooked** tum nâh gin jung; **he's a good cook** káo tum ah-hǎhn gèng

cooker dtao

cookie kóo-gêe

cool (*day, weather*) yen

cork (*in bottle*) jòok kòo-ut

corkscrew têe bpèrt kòo-ut

corn (*on foot*) dtah bplah

corner: **on the corner** (*of street*) hǒo-a moom; **in the corner** yòo dtrong hǒo-a mum; **a corner table** dtó mum

coronary (*noun*) hǒo-a jai wai

correct (*adjective*) tòok; **please correct me if I make a mistake** (*in speaking*) tâh pǒm (chún) pôot pìt chôo-ay gâir hâi dôo-ay

corridor tahng dern

corset gahng gayng rút sa-pôhk

cosmetics krêu-ung sǔm-ahng

cost rah-kah; **what does it cost?** rah-kah tâo-rài?

cot (*for baby*) bplay

cotton fâi

cotton buds (*for make-up removal etc*)

sǔm-lee bpùn hǒo
cotton wool sǔm-lee
couch têe nûng rúp kàirk
cough (*verb*) ai
cough tablets yah om kâir ai
cough medicine yah gâir ai
could: could you ...? koon ... dâi
mái?; **could I have ...?** kǒr ... dâi
mái?; **I couldn't ...** pǒm (chún) ...
mâi dâi
country (*nation*) bpra-tâyt
countryside chon-na-bòt
couple (*husband and wife*) sǎh-mee
pun-ra-yah kôo nèung; **a couple of
days** (*2-3 days*) sǒrng sǎhm wun
courier (*guide*) múk-koo-tâyt
course (*golf*) sa-nǎhm górp; (*of meal*)
chóot ah-hǎhn; **of course** nâir-norn;
of course not mâi ròrk
court (*law*) sǎhn; (*tennis*) sa-nǎhm
ten-nít
courtesy bus (*airport to hotel etc*) rót
bor-ri-gahn rúp sòng
cousin: my cousin yâht kǒrng pǒm
(chún)
cover charge 'cover charge'
cow woo-a
crab bpoo
crab fried rice kâo pùt bpoo
cracked: it's cracked (*plate etc*) dtàirk
cramp (*in leg etc*) nèp
crankshaft plao kôr wèe-ung
crash: there's been a car crash mee
rót chon gun
crash helmet mòo-uk gun nórk
crate lung; **can I have a crate of
Polaris** (*tm*) **water?** kǒr náhm poh-
la-rít lung nèung
crazy bâh
cream (*on milk, in cake, for face*) kreem
credit card bùt kray-dìt
crib (*baby's cot*) bplay
crisis chòok-chěrn
crisps mun fa-rùng tôrt
crockery tôo-ay chahm
crocodile jor-ra-kây
crook: he's a crook káo kêe gohng
crossing (*by sea*) kâhm ta-lay

crossroads sèe yâirk
crosswalk tahng máh lai
crowd fǒong kon; **there were crowds
of people** mee kon nâirn
crowded (*street, bars*) nâirn; **the bus
was crowded** rót may nâirn
crown (*on tooth*) lèe-um fun
crucial: it's absolutely crucial sǔm-
kun mâhk
cruise (*by ship*) lôrng reu-a
crutches mái yun rúk ráir
cry rórng hâi; **don't cry** yàh rórng
hâi nâ
cucumber dtairng gwah
cuisine: Thai cuisine ah-hǎhn tai
culture wút-ta-na-tum
cup tôo-ay; **a cup of coffee** gah-fair
tôo-ay nèung
cupboard dtôo
**cure: have you got something to
cure it?** mee yah gâir mái?
curlers krêu-ung dùt pǒm
current (*electrical*) gra-sǎir fai fáh; (*in
water*) gra-sǎir náhm
curry gairng; **beef curry** gairng néu-
a; **chicken curry** gairng gài; **Musul-
man curry** gairng mút-sa-mùn;
spicy curry gairng pèt
curtains mâhn
curve (*noun: in road*) hǒo-a kóhng
cushion mǒrn
custard apple nói nàh
custom bpra-pay-nee
Customs sǒon-la-gah-gorn
cut dtùt; **I've cut myself** pǒm (chún)
mee roy bàht; **could you cut a little
off here?** dtùt dtrong née òrk nít
nèung dâi mái?; **we were cut off**
(*telec*) tòok dtùt sǎi; **the engine
keeps cutting out** krêu-ung dùp
rêu-ay ler-ee
cutlery chórn sôrm
cycle: can we cycle there? (*is it far?*)
tèep jùk-gra-yahn bpai dâi mái?
cyclist kon tèep jùk-gra-yahn
cylinder (*of car*) sòop
cystitis gra-pór bpà-sǎh-wá ùk-sàyp

D

damage: you've damaged it koon tum hâi sěe-a; **it's damaged** mun sěe-a láir-o; **there's no damage** mâi mee a-rai sěe-a

damn! chìp-hǎi!

damp (*adjective*) chéun

dance (*verb*) dtên rum; **do you want to dance?** yàhk dtên rum mái?; **ramwong dance** (*popular Thai folk dance*) rum-wong

dancer: he's a good dancer káo dtên rum gèng

dancing: we'd like to go dancing rao yàhk bpai dtên rum; **Thai classical dancing** rum tai

dandruff kêe rung-kair

dangerous un-dta-rai

dare: I daren't pǒm (chún) mâi glâh

dark (*adjective*) dum; **dark blue** sěe núm ngern gàir; **when does it get dark?** mêut gèe mohng?; **after dark** dtorn kûm

darling têe rúk

dashboard pǎirng nâh bpùt

date: what's the date? wun née wun têe tâo-rài?; **on what date?** wun têe tâo-rài?; **can we make a date?** (*romantic, to business partner*) kǒr nút póp gun dâi mái?

dates (*to eat*) in-ta-pǎh-lum

daughter: my daughter lôok sǎo kǒrng pǒm (chún)

daughter-in-law lôok sa-pái

dawn (*noun*) rôong; **at dawn** rôong cháo

day wun; **the day after ...** wun lǔng jàhk têe ...; **the day before ...** wun gòrn ...; **every day** tóok wun; **one day** (*a single day*) wun nèung; **one day** (*in the future*) wun lǔng; **one day**

we'll meet again wun lǔng rao ja póp gun mài; **can we pay by the day?** rao jài bpen wun wun dâi mái?

daylight robbery (*extortionate prices*) pairng mâhk

day trip bpai glùp wun dee-o

dead dtai

deaf hǒo nòo-uk

deaf-aid krêu-ung chôo-ay fung

deal (*business*) tóo-ra-gìt; **it's a deal** (*agreed*) dtòk long láir-o; **will you deal with it?** chôo-ay tum hâi nòy dâi mái?

dealer (*agent*) ay-yen

dear (*expensive*) pairng

death kwahm dtai

December tun-wah-kom

decent: that's very decent of you koon jai dee mâhk

decide: we haven't decided yet rao yung mâi dâi dtùt sǐn jai; **you decide for us** chôo-ay dtùt sǐn jai hâi nòy; **it's all decided** (*arrangements made*) dtùt sǐn jai láir-o; (*agreement reached*) dtòk long gun láir-o

decision gahn dtùt sǐn jai

deck (*on ship*) dàht fáh

deckchair gâo êe pâh bai

declare: I have nothing to declare mây mee a-rai dtôrng sěe-a pah-sěe

decoration (*in room*) krêu-ung dtòp dtàirng

deduct hùk

deep léuk; **is it deep?** léuk mái?

deep-freeze (*noun*) châir kǎirng

definitely nâir-norn; **definitely not** mâi ròrk

degree (*university*) bpa-rin-yah; (*temperature*) ong-sǎh

dehydrated (*person*) sǒon sěe-a náhm

delay: the plane's arrival was delayed krêu-ung bin kâo cháh
deliberately doy-ee jay-dta-nah
delicacy: a Thai delicacy ah-hăhn pi-sàyt kŏrng tai
delicious a-ròy
delighted: delighted to meet you yin dee têe róo-jùk gun
deliver: will you deliver it? sòng bpai dâi mái?
delivery: is there another mail delivery? mee jòt-măi mah sòng èek mái?
de luxe pi-sàyt
denims gahng-gayng yeen
dent: there's a dent in it mee roy bÒop
dentist mŏr fun
dentures chóot fun tee-um
deny: he denies it káo bpà-dti-sàyt
deodorant yah dùp glìn dtoo-a
department store hâhng
departure kăh òrk
departure lounge hôrng pôo doy-ee săhn kăh òrk
depends: it depends láir-o dtàir; it depends on ... láir-o dtàir ...
deposit (downpayment) kâh mút-jum; to put down a deposit wahng kâh mút-jum; to deposit money in a bank fàhk ngern têe ta-na-kahn
depressed (mood) glÒom jai
depth kwahm léuk
describe bun-yai
deserted (beach, area) wâhng
dessert kŏrng wăhn
destination jÒot-măi bplai tahng
detergent pŏng súk fôrk
detour tahng ôrm
devalued: the dollar has been devalued kâh ngern dorn-lâh lót long
develop: could you develop these films? láhng feem née dâi mái?
diabetic: I'm a diabetic pŏm (chún) bpen rôhk bao wăhn; she's a diabetic káo bpen rôhk bao wăhn
diagram păirn-pŭng
dialect pah-săh tìn

dialling code ra-hùt toh-ra-sùp
diamond pét
diaper pâh ôrm
diarrhoea, diarrhea tórng sĕe-a; do you have something to stop diarrhoea? mee yah gâir tórng sĕe-a mái?
diary sa-mÒot bun-téuk bpra-jum wun
dictionary pót-ja-nah-nóo-grom; a Thai/English dictionary pót-ja-nah-nóo-grom tai ung-grìt
didn't see not and page 108
die dtai; I'm absolutely dying for a drink hĕw náhm ja dtai
diesel (fuel) núm mun rót dee-sen
diet: I'm on a diet pŏm (chún) gum-lung lót núm-nùk
difference kwahm dtàirk dtàhng; what's the difference between ...? ... dtàhng gun yung-ngai?; I can't tell the difference mâi hĕn mee kwahm dtàirk dtàhng a-rai; it doesn't make any difference mâi dtàhng a-rai gun ler-ee
different dtàhng; they are different dtàhng gun; they are very different dtàhng gun mâhk; it's different from this one dtàhng gùp un née; may we have a different table? kŏr bplèe-un dtó dâi mái?; ah well, that's different bpen kon la yàhng
difficult yâhk
difficulty (problem) bun-hăh; without any difficulty doy-ee mâi yâhk; I'm having difficulties with ... pŏm (chún) mee bun-hăh gùp ...
digestion gahn yôy ah-hăhn
dinghy reu-a bòt
dining car rót sa-bee-ung
dining room hôrng ah-hăhn
dinner ah-hăhn yen
dinner jacket sêu-a rah-dtree sa-moh-sŏrn
dinner party ngahn lée-ung ah-hăhn kûm
dipped headlights fai náh dtùm
dipstick têe wút núm mun krêu-ung
direct (adjective) dtrong; does it go

direct? wáir têe nǎi rěu bplào?

direction tahng; **in which direction is it?** yòo tahng nǎi?; **is it in this direction?** bpai tahng née, châi mái?

directory: telephone directory sa-mòot mǎi lâyk toh-ra-sùp

directory enquiries bor-ri-gahn sòrp tǎhm ber toh-ra-sùp

dirt kêe fòon

dirty (*hands, sheets, room, habit*) sòk-ga-bpròk

disabled pí-gahn

disagree: I disagree pǒm (chún) mâi hěn dôo-ay; **spicy food/seafood disagrees with me** pǒm (chún) gin ah-hǎhn pèt/ah-hǎhn ta-lay mâi bpen

disappear hǎi bpai; **it's simply disappeared** mun hǎi bpai nǎi gôr mâi róo

disappointed: I was disappointed pǒm (chún) pìt wǔng

disappointing mâi dee tâo têe kít wái

disaster hǎi-ya-ná

discharge (*pus*) mee núm nǒrng òrk

disc jockey dee-jay

disco dit-sa-gôh

disco dancing dit-sa-gôh dairn-sîng

discount: will you give me a discount? lót rah-kah hâi nòy, dâi mái?

disease rôhk

disgusting (*taste, food etc*) mâi ao nǎi

dish (*meal*) gùp kâo; (*plate*) jahn; (*bowl*) chahm

dishcloth pâh chét jahn

dishwashing liquid núm yah láhng chahm

disinfectant (*noun*) yah kâh chéu-a rôhk

disk of film feem déek

dislocated shoulder lài klêu-un

dispensing chemist ráhn kǎi yah

disposable nappies pâh ôrm têe chái láir-o tíng bpai ler-ee

distance ra-yá tahng; **what's the distance from ... to ...?** ... yòo hàhng jàhk ... gèe gee-loh?; **in the distance** yòo nai ra-yá glai

distilled water núm glùn

distributor (*in car*) môr grorng

district (*sub-division of province*) um-per

disturb: the disco is disturbing us sěe-ung dit-sa-gôh róp-goo-un rao

dive (*verb: into water*) dum náhm

diversion (*traffic*) bplèe-un sên tahng dern

divide (*share*) bàirng

diving board têe gra-dòht náhm

divorced yàh gun láir-o

dizzy: I feel dizzy pǒm (chún) wee-un hǒo-a; **dizzy spells** ah-gahn wee-un hǒo-a

do tum; **what shall I do?** pǒm (chún) ja tum yung-ngai?; **what are you doing tonight?** keun née koon tum a-rai?; **how do you do it?** tum yung-ngai?; **will you do it for me?** chôo-ay tum hâi nòy, dâi mái?; **who did it?** krai bpen kon tum?; **the meat's not done** néu-a yung mâi sòok; **what do you do?** (*job*) koon tum ngahn a-rai krúp (ká)?; **do you have ...?** mee ... mái?

docks tâh reu-a

doctor mǒr; **he needs to see a doctor** káo dtôrng bpai hǎh mǒr; **can you call a doctor?** chôo-ay rêe-uk mǒr hâi nòy dâi mái?

document àyk-ga-sǎhn

dog mǎh

doll dtóok-ga-dtah

dollar ngern dorn-lâh

don't! yàh; *see* **not** *and pages 108, 109*

door bpra-dtoo

doorman kon fâo bpra-dtoo

dosage wít-tee chái yah

double: double room hôrng kôo; **double bed** tee-ung yài; **double brandy** brùn-dee dup-bpern; **double r** (*in spelling name*) 'r' sǒrng dtoo-a; **it's all double Dutch to me** mâi róo rêu-ung ler-ee

doubt: I doubt it pǒm (chún) kít wâh kong mâi

doughnut doh-nút

down: get down! long bpai!, long mah!; **he's not down yet** (*is in room, bed*) káo yung mâi dâi long mah;

further on (down the road) ler-ee bpai èek; **I paid 20% down** pǒm (chún) wahng kâh mút-jum yêe-sìp bper-sen

downmarket (*restaurant, hotel*) rah-kah tòok

downstairs kâhng lâhng

dozen lǒh; **half a dozen** krêung lǒh

drain (*noun: in sink, street*) tôr ra-bai

draughts (*game*) màhk hórt

draughty: it's rather draughty mee lom yen kâo

draw (*picture*) wâht pâhp

drawing pin bpék

dreadful (*food, holiday, weather etc*) yâir

dream (*verb*) fǔn; **it's like a bad dream** (*this trip etc*) mun měu-un fǔn rái; **sweet dreams** fǔn wǎhn

dress (*woman's*) sêu-a chóot; **I'll just get dressed** děe-o bpai dtàirng dtoo-a gòrn

dressing (*for wound*) pâh pun plǎir; (*for salad*) núm (râht) sa-lùt

dressing gown sêu-a kloom chóot norn

drink (*verb*) dèum; **can I get you a drink?** kɔ͞on ja dèum a-rai mái?; **I don't drink** (*alcohol*) pǒm (chún) mâi dèum; **I must have something to drink** (*alcoholic or non-alcoholic*) pǒm (chún) yàhk gin náhm lěu-a gern; **a long cool drink** krêu-ung dèum yen yen; **may I have a drink of water?** kɔ̌r náhm gin nòy dâi mái?; **drink up!** dèum ray-o kâo!; **I had too much beer/whisky to drink** pǒm (chún) dèum bee-a/lâo mâhk gern bpai

drinkable: is the water drinkable? náhm née gin dâi mái?

drive: we drove here rao kùp rót mah; **I'll drive you home** pǒm

(chún) kùp rót bpai sòng; **do you want to come for a drive?** bpai nûng rót lên gun mái?; **is it a very long drive?** kùp rót bpai glai mái?

driver (*of car, bus*) kon kùp rót

driver's license bai kùp kèe

drive shaft sǎo kěm jò

driving licence bai kùp kèe

drizzle: it's drizzling fǒn dtòk prûm prûm

drop: just a drop please (*of drink*) kɔ̌r náhm súk yòt; **I dropped it** pǒm (chún) tum dtòk; **drop in some time** wun lǔng wáir mah hǎh

drown: he's drowning káo gum-lung jom náhm

drug (*medical*) yah; (*narcotic*) yah-sàyp-dtìt

drugstore ráhn kǎi yah

drunk (*adjective*) mao

drunken driving kùp rót ka-nà mao

dry (*adjective*) hâirng

dry-clean: can I get these dry-cleaned? súk-hâirng dâi mái?

dry-cleaner ráhn súk-hâirng

duck bpèt; **roast duck** bpèt yâhng; **duck rice** kâo nâh bpèt

due: when is the coach due? rót too-a kâo gèe mohng

dumb (*can't speak*) bpen bâi; (*stupid*) ngôh

dummy (*for baby*) hǒo-a nom lòrk

durex (*tm*) doo-rék

durian (*fruit*) tóo-ree-un

during nai ra-wàhng

dust fòon

dustbin tǔng ka-yà

duty (*customs*) pah-sěe

duty-free (*goods*) mâi dtôrng sěe-a pah-sěe

dynamo dai-nah-moh

dysentery rǒhk bìt

E

each: each of them (*people*) dtàir la kon; (*things*) dtàir la un; **one for each of us** kon la un; **how much are they each?** un la tâo-rài?; **each time** dtàir la krúng; **we know each other** rao róo-jùk gun

ear hǒo

earache: I have earache pǒm (chún) bpòo-ut hǒo

early (*arrive etc*) ray-o; **early in the morning** cháo dtròo; **it's too early** ray-o gern bpai; **a day earlier** gòrn wun nèung; **half an hour earlier** gòrn krêung chôo-a mohng; **I need an early night** pǒm (chún) dtôrng bpai norn dtàir hǒo-a kûm

early riser: I'm an early riser pǒm (chún) chôrp dtèun dtàir cháo

earring dtôom hǒo

earth (*soil*) din

earthenware krêu-ung bpûn din pǎo

east dta-wun òrk; **to the east** tahng dta-wun òrk

Easter ee-sa-dtêr

easy ngâi; **easy with the chilli!** yàh sài prík mâhk núk

eat (*informal word*) gin (kâo); (*polite, formal word*) tahn (kâo); **something to eat** kǒrng gin; **we've already eaten** rao gin kâo láir-o/rao tahn kâo láir-o

eau-de-Cologne núm hǒrm oh-di-koh-lohn

eccentric plǎirng

edible gin dâi

efficient (*hotel, organization*) mee bpra-sìt-ti-pâhp

egg kài

egg noodles ba-mèe

egg noodle soup ba-mèe náhm

eggplant ma-kěu-a

Eire ai-lairn

either: either ... or ... ... rěu ...; **I don't like either of them** pǒm (chún) mâi chôrp túng sǒrng yàhng

elastic (*noun*) sǎi yahng yêut

elastic band yahng rút

Elastoplast (*tm*) bplah-sa-dter

elbow kôr sòrk

electric fai fáh

electric cooker dtao fai fáh

electrician châhng fai fáh

electricity fai fáh

electric outlet chôrng bplúk

elegant ngahm sa-ngàh

elephant cháhng

elevator líf

else: something else a-rai èek; **somewhere else** têe èun; **let's go somewhere else** bpai têe èun mái?; **what else?** a-rai èek?; **nothing else, thanks** por láir-o, kòrp-kooN

embarrassed: he's embarrassed kěrn

embarrassing kěrn

embassy sa-tǎhn tôot

emergency chòok chěrn; **this is an emergency** bpen pah-wá chòok chěrn

emotional (*person*) jâo ah-rom

empty (*vacant*) wâhng (bplào); (*contents used up*) mòt láir-o

end (*verb*) sîn sòot, jòp; **when does it end?** jòp mêu-rài?; **at the end of the road** sòot ta-nǒn

energetic (*person*) gra-chôom gra-choo-ay

energy (*of person*) gum-lung

engaged (*to be married*) mûn; (*toilet*) mâi wâhng

engagement ring wǎirn mûn
engine krêu-ung yon
engine trouble krêu-ung yon dtìt kùt
England bpra-tâyt ung-grìt
English (*adjective*) ung-grìt; (*language*) pah-sǎh ung-grìt; **an English person/the English** kon ung-grìt; **I'm English** pǒm (chún) bpen kon ung-grìt; **do you speak English?** koon pôot pah-sǎh ung-grìt bpen mái?
Englishman pôo-chai ung-grìt
Englishwoman pôo-ying ung-grìt
enjoy: I enjoyed it very much pǒm (chún) chôrp mâhk; **enjoy yourself!** têe-o hâi sa-nòok
enjoyable sa-nòok dee
enlarge (*photo*) ka-yǎi
enormous yài bêr-rêr
enough por; **there's not enough** mâi por; **it's not big enough** yài mâi por; **thank you, that's enough** kòrp-koon, por láir-o
entertainment kwahm bun-terng
entrance (*noun*) tahng kâo
envelope sorng jòt-mǎi
epileptic bpen lom bâh mǒo
equipment òop-bpa-gorn; (*in apartment*) krêu-ung chái sǒy
eraser yahng lóp
error têe pìt
escalator bun-dai lêu-un
especially doy-ee cha-pór
espresso coffee gah-fair èt-sa-bpret-soh
essential: it is essential that ... jum-bpen têe ...
estate agent ay-yên kǎi bâhn
ethnic minority chon glòom nói
Europe yóo-rôhp
European (*noun*) chao yóo-rôhp; (*any Caucasian*) fa-rùng
European-style bàirp fa-rùng
even: even the English máir dtàir kon ung-grìt; **even if ...** máir wâh ...
evening dtorn glahng keun; **good evening** sa-wùt dee; **this evening** (*until 6 o'clock*) yen née; (*after that*) keun née; **in the evening** (*until 6

o'clock) dtorn yen; (*after that*) dtorn glahng keun; **evening meal** ah-hǎhn yen
evening dress (*for men*) chóot yài; (*for woman*) chòot rah-dtree
eventually nai têe sòot
ever: have you ever been to ...? koon ker-ee bpai ... mái?; **if you ever come to Britain ...** tâh koon dâi bpai bpra-tâyt ung-grìt la kôr ...
every tóok; **every day** tóok wun
everyone tóok kon
everything tóok yàhng
everywhere tôo-a bpai
exactly! châi láir-o!
exam gahn sòrp
examine (*inspect*) dtròo-ut
example dtoo-a yàhng; **for example ...** chên ...
excellent (*food, hotel*) yêe-um; **excellent!** yêe-um ler-ee!
except yók wáyn; **except Sunday** yók wáyn wun ah-tít
exception kôr yók wáyn; **as an exception** bpen kôr yók wáyn
excess baggage núm-nùk gern
excessive mâhk bpai; **that's a bit excessive** mâhk bpai nòy
exchange (*verb: money*) lâirk bplèe-un; **in exchange** lâirk bplèe-un
exchange rate: what's the exchange rate? ùt-dtrah lâirk bplèe-un tâo-rài?
exciting (*day, holiday, film*) nâh dtèun dtên
exclusive (*club, hotel*) chún nèung
excursion bor-ri-gahn num têe-o; **is there an excursion to ...?** mee bor-ri-gahn num têe-o ... mái?
excuse me (*to get past*) kǒr-tôht; (*to get attention*) koon krúp (kâ); (*pardon?*) a-rai ná krúp (ká); (*annoyed*) kǒr-tôht
exhaust (*on car*) tôr ay sěe-a
exhausted (*tired*) nèu-ay
exhibition nít-tá-sa-gahn
exist: does it still exist? yung mee yòo mái?
exit tahng òrk
expect: I expect so pǒm (chún) kít

wâh yung ngún; **she's expecting** káo
mee tórng
expenses kâh chái jài
expensive pairng
experience bpra-sòp-ba-gahn; **an
absolutely unforgettable experience**
bpen bpra-sòp-ba-gahn têe mâi mee
wun leum
experienced mee bpra-sòp-ba-gahn
expert pôo chêe-o chahn
expire: it's expired (*passport etc*) mòt
ah-yóo
explain a-ti-bai; **would you explain
that to me?** chôo-ay a-ti-bai hâi nòy,
dâi mái?
explore sǔm-ròo-ut; **I just want to go
and explore** pǒm (chún) yàhk ja
bpai têe-o sǔm-ròo-ut doo
export (*verb*) sòng òrk
exposure meter krêu-ung wút sǎirng

express (*mail*) bprai-sa-nee dòo-un;
(*train*) rót fai dòo-un
extra: can we have an extra chair?
kǒr gâo êe pêrm èek dtoo-a nèung;
is that extra? (*in cost*) kít dtàhng
hàhk rěu bplào?
**extraordinarily: extraordinarily
beautiful** sǒo-ay lěu-a gern
extraordinary (*very strange*) bplàirk
mâhk
extremely mâhk lěu-a gern
extrovert chôrp sa-dairng òrk
eye dtah; **will you keep an eye on
my bags for me?** chôo-ay fâo gra-
bpǎo hâi pǒm (chún) nòy, dâi mái?
eyebrow kéw
eyebrow pencil din-sǒr kěe-un kéw
eye drops yah yòrt dtah
eye shadow kreem tah nǔng dtah
eye witness pa-yahn

F

fabulous yôrt
face nâh
face mask (*for diving*) nâh gàhk gun
náhm
face pack (*cosmetic*) chóot dtàirng nâh
facing: facing the sea hǔn bpai tahng
ta-lay
fact kôr tét jing
factory rohng ngahn
Fahrenheit fair-ren-háit; *see page 115*
faint: she's fainted káo bpen lom;
I'm going to faint pǒm (chún)
gum-lung ja bpen lom
fair (*festival*) ngahn; (*commercial*)
ngahn sa-dairng sǐn-káh; **it's not fair**
mâi yóot-dti-tum; **OK, fair enough**
oh kay, dtòk long
fake kǒrng bplorm
fall: he's had a fall káo hòk lóm; **he
fell off his bike** káo dtòk jùk-gra-

yahn; **in the fall** (*autumn*) reu-doo
bai mái rôo-ung
false mâi jing
false teeth chóot fun tee-um
family krôrp-kroo-a
family name nahm sa-goon
famished: I'm famished pǒm (chún)
hěw jung ler-ee
famous mee chêu sěe-ung
fan (*mechanical*) pút lom; (*hand held*)
pút; (*football fan*) fairn fóot-born
fan belt sǎi pahn
fancy: he fancies you káo chôrp
koon
fancy dress party ngahn dtàirng
fairn-sêe
fantastic wí-sàyt jung ler-ee
far glai; **is it far?** yòo glai mái?; **how
far is it to ...?** ... glai jàhk têe nêe
gèe gi-loh?; **as far as I'm concerned**

... sòo-un pŏm (chún) ...

fare kâh doy-ee săhn; **what's the fare to ...?** kâh doy-ee săhn bpai ... tâo-rài?

farewell party ngahn lée-ung sòng

farm fahm

farmer (*of rice*) chao nah

farther glai gwàh; **farther than ...** glai gwàh ...

fashion (*in clothes etc*) fair-chûn

fashionable tun sa-măi

fast ray-o; **not so fast** yàh hâi ray-o núk

fastener (*on clothes*) sâi rút

fat (*person*) ôo-un; (*on meat*) mun

father pôr; **my father** pôr kŏrng pŏm (chún)

father-in-law (*of a man*) pôr dtah; (*of a woman*) pôr pŏo-a

fattening: it's fattening tum hâi ôo-un

faucet górk náhm

fault kwahm pìt; **it was my fault** kwahm pìt kŏrng pŏm (chún); **it's not my fault** mâi châi kwahm pìt kŏrng pŏm (chún)

faulty (*equipment*) sĕe-a

favo(u)rite kŏrng bpròht; **that's my favo(u)rite** bpen kŏrng bpròht kŏrng pŏm (chún)

fawn (*colour*) sĕe tao gairm lĕu-ung

fear (*verb*) gloo-a

February goom-pah-pun

fed up: I'm fed up pŏm (chún) bèu-a; **I'm fed up with ...** pŏm (chún) bèu-a ...

feeding bottle kòo-ut nom

feel róo-sèuk; **I feel hot/cold** pŏm (chún) róo-sèuk rórn/năo; **I feel like a drink** pŏm (chún) yàhk gin náhm; **I don't feel like going** pŏm (chún) mâi yàhk bpai; **how are you feeling today?** róo-sèuk bpen yung-ngai bâhng wun née?; **I'm feeling a lot better** pŏm róo-sèuk kôy yung chôo-a kêun mâhk

fence róo-a

fender (*of car*) gun chon

ferry reu-a kâhm fâhk; **what time's the last ferry?** reu-a kâhm fâhk têe-o sòot tái òrk gèe mohng?

festival ngahn

fetch: I'll go and fetch it pŏm (chún) ja bpai ao mah; **will you come and fetch me?** mah rúp pŏm (chún) dâi mái?

fever kâi

feverish: I'm feeling feverish pŏm (chún) bpen kâi

few: only a few lék nóy; **a few minutes** mâi gèe nah-tee; **he's had a good few (to drink)** káo dèum kâo bpai mâhk láir-o

fiancé: my fiancé kôo mûn kŏrng chún

fiancée: my fiancée kôo mûn kŏrng pŏm

fiasco: what a fiasco! mâi ao năy!

field (*rice, paddy*) nah; (*sport*) sa-năhm

fifty-fifty hâh-sìp hâh-sìp

fight (*noun*) gahn chók dtòy

figure (*of person*) rôop-song; (*number*) măi-lâyk; **I have to watch my figure** pŏm (chún) dtôrng rúk-săh rôop-song

fill dterm; **fill her up please** (*with petrol*) dterm núm mun hâi dtem; **will you help me fill out this form?** chôo-ay pŏm (chún) gròrk form nòy, dâi mái?

fillet néu-a sŭn

filling (*in tooth*) òot fun; **it's very filling** (*food*) gin láir-o ìm

filling station bpúm núm mun

film (*in cinema*) năng; (*for camera*) feem; **shall we go and see a film?** bpai doo năng mái?; **do you have this type of film?** mee feem bàirp née mái?; **16mm film** feem sìp hòk min-li-mét; **35mm film** feem săhm sìp hâh min-li-mét

filter (*for camera*) fin-dter; (*for coffee*) krêu-ung grorng

filter-tipped gôn grorng

filthy (*room etc*) sòk-ga-bpròk

find jer; **I can't find it** pŏm (chún) hăh mâi jer; **if you find it** tâh hăh jer; **I've found a ...** pŏm (chún) jer

... láir-o

fine: it's fine weather ah-gàht dee; **a 500 baht fine** kâh bprùp hâh róy bàht; **how are you? — fine thanks** bpen yung ngai bâhng? — sa-bai dee kòrp-koon mâhk

finger néw meu

fingernail lép meu

finish: I haven't finished pǒm (chún) yung mâi sèt; **when I've finished** way-lah pǒm (chún) sèt láir-o; **when does the film finish?** nǔng lêrk gèe mohng?; **finish off your drink** dèum sěe-a hâi mòt

fire: fire! (something's on fire) fai mâi!; **may we light a fire here?** gòr fai dtrong née dâi mái?; **it's on fire** fai mâi; **it's not firing properly** (car) krêu-ung tum ngahn mâi dee

fire alarm sǔn-yahn fay mâi

fire brigade, fire department gorng dtum-ròo-ut dùp plerng

fire escape bun-dai sǔm-rùp něe fai

fire extinguisher krêu-ung dùp plerng

firm (company) bor-ri-sùt

first râirk; **I was first** pǒm (chún) bpen kon râirk; **at first** tee râirk; **this is the first time** krúng née bpen krúng râirk

first aid gahn bpa-tǒm pa-yah-bahn

first aid kit chóot bpa-tǒm pa-yah-bahn

first class (travel etc) chún nèung

first name chêu

fish (noun) bplah

fisherman kon jùp bplah

fishing jùp bplah

fishing boat reu-a bpra-mong

fishing net hǎir

fishing rod kun bpèt

fishing tackle tôon bpèt

fishing village mòo bâhn bpra-mong

fit (healthy) sòok-ka-pâhp sǒm-boon; **I'm not very fit** pǒm (chún) róo-sèuk sòok-ka-pâhp mâi kôy sǒm-boon; **he's a keep fit fanatic** káo bpen rôhk bâh òrk gum-lung; **it doesn't fit** mun mâi kâo gun

fix: can you fix it? (mend) gâir dâi mái?; **let's fix a time** nút way-lah máy?; **it's all fixed up** jùt gahn rêe-up róy láir-o; **I'm in a bit of a fix** mee bpun-hǎh nòy

fizzy sâh

fizzy drink núm ùt lom

flabby (body) yòrn yahn

flag tong

flannel pâh chét nâh

flash (for camera) fláirt

flashlight fai chǎi

flashy (clothes etc) rǒo rǎh

flat (adjective) bairn; **this beer is flat** bee-a jèut; **I've got a flat tyre/tire** yahng bairn; (apartment) fláirt

flatterer bpàhk wǎhn

flatware (cutlery) chórn sôrm; (crockery) tôo-ay chahm

flavo(u)r rót

flea mùt

flea bite mùt gùt

flexible (material, arrangements) yêut yòon dâi

flies (on trousers) síp

flight têe-o bin

flippers rorng tâo ma-nóot gòp

flirt (noun) kon jâo chóo

float loy

floating market dta-làht náhm

flood náhm tôo-um; **does it flood here in the rainy season?** nâh fǒn náhm tôo-um têe nêe rěu bplào?

floor (of room) péun; **on the floor** yòo bon péun; **on the second floor** (UK) chún sǎhm; (USA) chún sǒrng

floorshow flor-choh

flop (failure) lóm lǎy-o

florist ráhn kǎi dòrk-mái

flour bpâirng sǎh-lee

flower dòrk-mái

flu kâi wùt

fluent klôrng; **he speaks fluent Thai** káo pôot pah-sǎh tai dâi klôrng

fly (verb) bin; **can we fly there?** bin bpai dâi mái?

fly (insect) ma-lairng wun

fly spray yah chèet ma-lairng

foggy: it's foggy mòrk long

fog lights fai mòrk
folk dancing gahn fórn rum péun meu-ung
folk music don-dtree péun meu-ung
follow dtahm; **follow me** dtahm pŏm (chún) mah
fond: I'm quite fond of ... pŏm (chún) chôrp ...
food ah-hăhn; **the food's excellent** ah-hăhn a-ròy dee
food poisoning ah-hăhn bpen pít
food store ráhn kăi kŏrng chum
fool kon ngôh
foolish ngôh
foot táo; **on foot** dern bpai; *see page 113*
football (*game, ball*) fóot-born
for: for her sŭm-rùp káo; **is that for me?** nûn sŭm-rùp pŏm (chún) châi mái?; **what's this for?** nêe sŭm-rùp a-rai?; **for two days** sŏrng wun; **I've been here for a week** pŏm (chún) yòo têe nêe ah-tít nèung láir-o; **a bus for ...** rót-may bpai ...
forbidden hâhm
forehead nâh pàhk
foreign dtàhng bpra-tâyt
foreigner chao dtàhng bpra-tâyt
foreign exchange (*money*) ngern dtàhng bpra-tâyt; (*place*) têe lâirk bplèe-un ngern dtrah dtàhng bpra-tâyt
forest bpàh
forget leum; **I forget, I've forgotten** pŏm (chún) leum bpai láir-o; **don't forget** yàh leum ná
fork (*for eating*) sôrm; (*in road*) tahng yâirk
form (*in hotel, to fill out*) bàirb form
formal (*dress, person, language*) bpen tahng gahn
fortnight sŏrng ah-tít
fortunately chôhk dee
fortune-teller mŏr doo
forward: could you forward my mail? chôo-ay sòng jòt-măi dtòr bpai hâi dôo-ay
foundation cream kreem rorng péun
fountain (*ornamental, for drinking*)

núm póo
fracture (*noun*) gra-dòok hùk
fractured skull gra-lòhk sĕe-sà dtàirk
fragile dtàirk ngâi; **fragile — handle with care** ra-wung kŏrng dtàirk
frame (*for picture*) gròrp rôop
France bpra-tâyt fa-rùng-sàyt
fraud gohng
free (*at liberty, costing nothing*) free; **admission free** mâi gèp kâh pàhn bpra-dtoo, free
freezer dtôo châir kăirng
freezing cold: this room is freezing cold hôrng née năo ja dtai
French (*adjective*) fa-rùng-sàyt; (*language*) pah-săh fa-rùng-sàyt; **a French person/the French** kon fa-rùng-sàyt
French fries mun fa-rùng tôrt
frequent bòi bòi
fresh (*weather, breeze*) sòt chêun; (*fruit etc*) sòt; (*cheeky*) yôong; **don't get fresh with me** yàh mah yôong gùp chún
fresh orange juice núm sôm kún
friction tape pâh táyp
Friday wun sòok
fridge dtôo yen
fried egg kài dao
fried rice kâo pùt
friend pêu-un
friendly bpen pêu-un
frog gòp
from jàhk; **I'm from ...** pŏm (chún) mah jàhk ...; **where are you from?** koon mah jàhk năi?; **from here to the sea** jàhk têe nêe tĕung ta-lay; **the next boat from ...** reu-a jàhk ... têe-o nâh; **as from Tuesday** dtûng dtàir wun ung-kahn bpen dtôn bpai
front nâh; **in front** kâhng nâh; **in front of us** kâhng nâh rao; **at the front** kâhng nâh
frozen châir kăirng
frozen food ah-hăhn châir kăirng
fruit pŏn-la-mái
fruit juice núm pŏn-la-mái
fruit salad sa-lùt pŏn-la-mái
frustrating: it's very frustrating

yôong mâhk

fry (*deep fry*) tôrt; (*stir fry*) pùt; **I can't eat anything fried** pŏm (chún) gin ah-hăhn tôrt réu pùt mâi bpen

frying pan ga-tá

full dtem láir-o; **it's full of ...** dtem bpai dôo-ay ...; **I'm full** (*eating*) pŏm (chún) ìm láir-o

full-board gin yòo prórm

fun: it's fun sa-nòok dee; **it was great fun** sa-nòok dee mâhk; **just for fun** lên sa-nòok sa-nòok; **have fun** sa-nòok na

funeral ngahn sòp

funny (*strange*) bplàirk; (*amusing*) dta-lòk

furniture krêu-ung reu-un

further ler-ee bpai; **2 kilometres further** ler-ee bpai èek sŏrng gi-loh; **further down the road** ler-ee bpai èek

fuse (*noun*) few; **the lights have fused** few kàht

fuse wire săi few

future a-nah-kót; **in future** nai a-nah-kót

G

gale pah-yóo

gallon gairn-lun; *see page 115*

gallstones nêw núm dee

gamble pa-nun; **I don't gamble** pŏm (chún) mâi chôrp lên gahn pa-nun

game gaym

garage (*petrol*) púm núm mun; (*for repairs*) òo sôrm rót; (*for parking*) rohng rót

garbage ka-yà

garden sŏo-un

garlic gra-tee-um

gas gáirt; (*gasoline*) núm mun gáht

gas cylinder (*for Calor gas*) tŭng gáirt

gas pedal kun rêng

gas station púm núm mun

gas tank tŭng núm mun

gastroenteritis gra-pór ùk-sàyp

gate bpra-dtoo; (*at airport*) chôrng kâo

gauge krêu-ung wút

gay (*homosexual*) gra-ter-ee

gear gee-a; **the gears keep sticking** gee-a fèut

gearbox glòrng gee-a; **I have gearbox trouble** glòrng gee-a sĕe-a

gear lever, gear shift kun gee-a

general delivery ' poste restante'

generous: that's very generous of you koon jai-dee mâhk

gentleman (*man*) soo-pâhp boo-ròot; **that gentleman over there** pôo-chai kon nóhn; **he's such a gentleman** káo bpen soo-pâhp boo-ròot jing jing

gents (*toilet*) hôrng náhm pôo-chai

genuine táir

German (*adjective*) yer-ra-mun; (*language*) pah-săh yer-ra-mun; **a German/the Germans** kon yer-ra-mun

German measles rôhk hùt yer-ra-mun

Germany bpra-tâyt yer-ra-mun

get: have you got ...? mee ... mái?; **how do I get to ...?** bpai ... yung ngai?; **where do I get it from?** pŏm (chún) ao mah jàhk têe năi?; **can I get you a drink?** ja dèum a-rai mái?; **will you get it for me?** chôo-ay ao hâi pŏm (chún) nòy dâi mái?; **when do we get there?** rao ja bpai tĕung mêu-a rài?; **I've got to ...** pŏm (chún) dtôrng ...; **I've got to go** pŏm (chún) dtôrng bpai; **where do I**

get off? pǒm (chún) long têe nǎi?;
it's difficult to get to bpai lum-bàhk;
when I get up (*in morning*) way-lah
pǒm (chún) dtèun
ghastly nâh glèe-ut
ghost pěe
giddy: it makes me giddy tum hâi
pǒm (chún) wee-un hǒo-a
gift kǒrng kwǔn
gigantic yài bêr-rêr
gin lâo yin; **a gin and tonic** yin toh-
nik
girl pôo-yǐng
girlfriend fairn
give hâi; **will you give me ...?** ja hâi
... pǒm (chún) mái?; **I'll give you
100 baht** pǒm (chún) ja hâi koon
róy bàht; **I gave it to him** pǒm
(chún) hâi káo bpai láir-o; **will you
give it back?** koon ja keun hâi mái?;
would you give this to ...? chôo-ay
ao née bpai hâi ... nòy, dâi mái?
glad yin dee
glamorous (*woman*) rǒo-rǎh-fôo-fâh
gland dtòrm
glandular fever dtòrm núm lěu-ung
bpen pít
glass (*material*) gâir-o; (*drinking*) gâir-
o; **a glass of water** gâir-o náhm
glasses (*spectacles*) wâirn dtah
gloves tǒong meu
glue (*noun*) gao
gnat rín
go bpai; **we want to go to ...** rao yàhk
ja bpai ...; **I'm going there
tomorrow** pǒm (chún) bpai prôong
née; **when does it go?** (*bus etc*) òrk
mêu-a rài?; **where are you going?**
bpai nǎi?; **let's go** bpai tèr; **he's
gone** káo bpai láir-o; **it's all gone**
mòt láir-o; **I went there yesterday**
pǒm (chún) bpai mêu-a wahn née;
fried rice to go kǒr kâo pùt sài hòr;
go away! bpai hâi pón!; **it's gone off**
(*milk etc*) sěe-a láir-o; **we're going
out tonight** keun née rao bpai têe-o;
do you want to go out tonight?
keun née yàhk bpai têe-o mái?; **has
the price gone up?** rah-kah kêun

rěu bplào?
goal (*sport*) bpra-dtoo
goat pái
God pra-jâo
gold torng
Golden Triangle sǎhm lěe-um torng
kum
goldsmith châhng torng
golf górp
golf clubs mái górp
golf course sa-nǎhm górp
gong kórng
good dee; **good!** dee!; **that's no good**
mâi dee; **good heavens!** tôh!
goodbye lah gòrn ná
good-looking lòr
goose hàhn
gorgeous (*meal*) a-ròy mâhk; (*woman*)
sǒo-ay mâhk
government rút-ta-bahn
government employee kâh-râht-cha-
gahn
gradually tee la nóy
grammar wai-yah-gorn
gram(me) grum; *see page 113*
granddaughter lǎhn sǎo
grandfather (*paternal*) bpòo; (*maternal*)
dtah
grandmother (*paternal*) yâh; (*maternal*)
yai
grandson lǎhn chai
grapes a-ngòon
grass yâh
grateful bpen nêe boon-koon;
I'm very grateful to you pǒm
(chún) róo-sèuk bpen nêe boon-
koon koon
gray sěe tao
grease (*for car*) núm mun; (*on food*)
kǎi mun
greasy (*food*) mun
great: that's great! yôrt!
Great Britain bpra-tâyt ung-grìt
greedy dta-gla
green sěe kěe-o
greengrocer ráhn kǎi pùk
grey sěe tao
grilled yâhng
gristle (*on meat*) pung pèut

grocer ráhn kǎi kǒrng chum
grotto tûm
ground péun din; **on the ground** bon péun din; **on the ground floor** chún nèung
ground beef néu-a sùp
group pôo-uk
group insurance bpra-gun chee-wít glòom
group leader (*on tour*) pôo num têe-o
guarantee (*noun*) bai rúp bpra-gun; **is it guaranteed?** mee bai rúp bpra-gun mái?

guardian (*of child*) pôo bpòk-krorng
guest kàirk
guest house gáyt háot
guide (*noun*) múk-koo-tâyt
guidebook kôo meu num têe-o
guilty mee kwahm pìt
guitar gee-dtâh
Gulf of Siam ào tai
gum (*in mouth*) ngèu-uk; (*chewing gum*) màhk fa-rùng
gun bpeun
gymnasium rohng yim
gyn(a)ecologist na-ree pâirt

H

hair (*on the head*) pǒm; (*on the body*) kǒn
hairbrush bprairng pǒm
haircut dtùt pǒm; **just an ordinary haircut please** dtùt bàirp tum-ma-dah ná
hairdresser châhng dùt pǒm
hairdryer krêu-ung bpào pǒm
hair grip gíp nèp pǒm
half krêung; **half an hour** krêung chôo-a mohng; **a half portion** krêung sòo-un; **half a litre/liter** krêung lít; **half as much** krêung nèung; *see page 111*
halfway: halfway to Bangkok krêung tahng groong-tâyp
ham mǒo hairm
hamburger hairm-ber-gêr
hammer (*noun*) kórn
hand meu; **will you give me a hand?** mah chôo-ay pǒm (chún) nòy, dâi mái?
handbag gra-bpǎo tǔu
hand baggage gra-bpǎo tǔu
handbrake brayk meu
handkerchief pâh chét nâh
handle (*noun*) dâhm; **will you handle**

it? chôo-ay jùt gahn nâi nòy, dâi mái?
hand luggage gra-bpǎo tǔu
handmade tum dôo-ay meu
handsome rôop lòr
hanger (*for clothes*) mái kwǎirn sêu-a
hangover bpòo-ut hǒo-a; **I've got a terrible hangover** pǒm (chún) bpòo-ut hǒo-a mâhk
happen gèrt kêun; **how did it happen?** mun gèrt kêun dâi yung ngai?; **what's happening?** gèrt a-rai kêun?; **it won't happen again** ja mâi gèrt kêun èek
happy dee jai; **we're not happy with the room** rao mâi kôy chôrp hôrng née
harbo(u)r tâh reu-a
hard (*not soft*) kǎirng; (*difficult*) yâhk
hard-boiled egg kài dtôm kǎirng
hard lenses láyn kǎirng
hardly mâi kôy ...; **I hardly ever drink alcohol** pǒm (chún) mâi kôy gin lâo
hardware store ráhn kǎi krêu-ung lèk
harm (*noun*) un-dta-rai

hassle: it's too much hassle yôong mâhk gern bpai; **a hassle-free trip** gahn dern tahng têe mâi yôong yâhk

hat mòo-uk

hate: I hate ... pǒm (chún) glèe-ut ...

have mee; **do you have ...?** mee ... mái?; **can I have ...?** kǒr ... nòy?; **can I have some water?** kǒr náhm nòy dâi mái?; **I have ...** pǒm (chún) mee ...; **I don't have ...** pǒm (chún) mâi mee ...; **can we have breakfast in our room?** gin ah-hǎhn cháo nai hôrng rao, dâi mái?; **have another** ao èek un si; **I have to leave early** pǒm (chún) dtôrng bpai ray-o; **do I have to ...?** pǒm (chún) dtôrng ... rěu bplào?; **do we have to ...?** rao dtôrng ... rěu bplào?

hay fever rôhk hèut

he káo; **is he here?** káo yòo têe nêe mái?; **where does he live?** káo púk yòo têe nǎi?; *see page 101*

head hǒo-a; **we're heading for Chiangmai** rao ja bpai chee-ung mài

headache bpòo-ut hǒo-a

headlights fai nâh rót

headphones hǒo fung

head wind lom dtâhn

health sòok-ka-pâhp

healthy (*person*) mee sòok-ka-pâhp dee; (*food*) bpen bpra-yòht gàir râhng-gai; **healthy climate** ah-gàht bor-ri-sòot

hear: can you hear me? dâi yin mái?; **I can't hear you** pǒm (chún) mâi dâi yin; **I've heard about it** pǒm (chún) ker-ee dâi yin

hearing aid krêu-ung chôo-ay fung

heart hǒo-a jai

heart attack hǒo-a jai wai

heat kwahm rórn; **not in this heat!** rórn yàhng née mâi ao!

heated rollers krêu-ung móo-un pǒm fai fáh

heating krêu-ung tum kwahm rórn

heat rash bpen pèun

heat stroke páir dàirt

heavy nùk

hectic chòok-la-hòok

heel (*of foot*) sôn táo; (*of shoe*) sôn rorng táo; **could you put new heels on these?** bplèe-un sôn mài hâi nòy, dâi mái?

height (*of person, of mountain*) kwahm sǒong

helicopter hay-li-kòrp-dtêr

hell: oh hell! dtai hàh!

hello (*said by man*) sa-wùt dee krúp; (*said by woman*) sa-wùt dee kâ; (*in surprise*) oh-hǒh; (*on phone*) hun-loh

helmet (*for motorcycle*) moo-ùk gun chon

help (*verb*) chôo-ay; **can you help me?** chôo-ay pǒm (chún) nòy, dâi mái?; **thanks for your help** kòrp-koon têe dâi chôo-ay lěu-a; **help!** chôo-ay dôo-ay!

helpful: he was very helpful káo chôo-ay lěu-a pǒm (chún) dee mâhk; **that's helpful** bpen bpra-yòht mâhk

hepatitis dtùp ùk-sàyp

her káo; **I don't know her** pǒm (chún) mâi róo-jùk káo; **can you send it to her?** chôo-ay sông bpai hâi káo, dâi mái?; **it's her** káo ayng; **with her** gùp káo; **for her** sǔm-rùp káo; **that's her suitcase** nûn gra-bpǎo kǒrng káo; *see pages 100, 101*

herbs krêu-ung tâyt

here têe nêe; **here you are** (*giving something*) nêe ngai; **here he comes** mah láir-o

hers kǒrng káo; **that's hers** nún kǒrng káo; *see page 102*

hey! háy!

hi! bpai nǎi?

hiccups sa-èuk

hide (*verb*) sôrn

hideous (*taste, weather, journey*) nâh glèe-ut

high sǒong

highbeam fai sǒong

highchair gâo êe sǒong

highway tahng lǒo-ung

hill kǎo; **it's further up the hill** ler-ee kǎo bpai èek

hillside cherng kǎo

hill tribe chao kǎo

hilly bpen nern

him káo; **I don't know him** pǒm (chún) mâi róo-jùk káo; **can you send it to him?** chôo-ay sòng bpai hâi káo, dâi mái?; **it's him** káo ayng; **with him** gùp káo; **for him** sǔm-rùp káo; *see page 101*

hip sa-pôhk

hire châo; **can I hire a car?** mee rót hâi châo mái?; **do you hire them out?** mee hâi châo mái?

his kǒrng káo; **it's his drink** krêu-ung dèum kǒrng káo; **it's his** kǒrng káo; *see pages 100, 102*

history bpra-wùt-sàht; **the history of Thailand** bpra-wùt-sàht bpra-tâyt tai

hit dtee; **he hit me** káo dtee pǒm (chún); **I hit my head** pǒm (chún) hǒo-a chon

hitch: is there a hitch? mee bpun-hǎh mái?

hitch-hike bòhk rót

hit record playng hít

hole roo

holiday wun yòot; **I'm on holiday** pǒm (chún) yòot púk pòrn

home bâhn; **at home** (*in my house etc*) têe bâhn; (*in my country*) nai bpra-tâyt rao; **I go home tomorrow** pǒm (chún) glùp bâhn prôong née

home address têe yòo têe bâhn

homemade tum têe bâhn

homesick: I'm homesick pǒm (chún) kít těung bâhn

homosexual gra-ter-ee

honest sêu dtrong

honestly? jing jing lěr?

honey núm pêung

honeymoon hun-nee-moon; **it's our honeymoon** rao hun-nee-moon gun

hood (*of car*) gra-bprohng rót

hope (*verb*) wǔng; **I hope so** wǔng wâh yung ngún; **I hope not** wǔng wâh kông mâi

horn (*of car*) dtrair

horrible yâir mâhk

horse máh

horse riding kèe máh

hose (*for car radiator*) tôr yahng

hospital rohng pa-yah-bahn

hospitality gahn dtôrn rúp kùp sôo; **thank you for your hospitality** kòrp-koon têe dtôrn rúp kùp sôo

hostess (*in bar*) pôo-yǐng bah

hot (*in temperature*) rórn; (*with spices*) pèt; **I'm hot** pǒm (chún) rórn; **it's so hot today** wun née ah-gàht rórn jung ler-ee

hotdog hórt dórg

hotel rohng rairm; **at my hotel** têe rohng rairm pǒm (chún)

hotel clerk (*receptionist*) pa-núk ngahn dtôrn rúp bpra-jum rohng rairm

hour chôo-a mohng; **on the hour** dtrong chôo-a mohng

house bâhn

housewife mâir bâhn

how: how ...? yung ngai?; **how many ...?** gèe ...?; **how much?** tâo-rài?; **how often?** bòy mái?; **how are you?** bpen yung ngai bâhng?; **how do you do?** sa-wùt dee krúp (kâ); **how about a beer?** gin bee-a mái?; **how nice!** dee jung ná!; **would you show me how to?** bòrk dâi mái wâh tum yung ngai?

humid chéun

humidity kwahm chéun

humo(u)r: where's your sense of humo(u)r? ah-rom kǔn kǒrng koon hǎi bpai nǎi?

hundredweight *see page 114*

hungry: I'm hungry pǒm (chún) hěw; **I'm not hungry** pǒm (chún) mâi hěw

hurry: I'm in a hurry pǒm (chún) dtôrng rêep; **hurry up!** rêep rêep nòy!; **there's no hurry** mâi dtôrng rêep

hurt: it hurts jèp; **my back hurts** jèp lǔng

husband sǎh-mee; **my husband** sǎh-mee kǒrng chún

I

I (*male*) pŏm; (*female*) chún; **I'm English** pŏm (chún) bpen kon ung-grìt; **I live in Manchester** pŏm (chún) yòo têe Manchester; *see page 101*
ice núm kăirng; **with ice** sài núm kăirng; **with ice and lemon** sài núm kăirng gùp ma-nao
ice cream ai-sa-kreem
iced coffee gah-fair yen
ice lolly ai-sa-kreem tâirng
idea kwahm kít; **good idea!** châi láir-o
ideal (*solution, time*) mòr
identity card bùt bpra-jum dtoo-a
idiot kon bâh
idyllic ngót-ngahm
if tâh; **if you could** tâh bpen bpai dâi; **if not** tâh mâi yung ngún
ignition bpòom dùt krêu-ung
ill mâi sa-bai; **I feel ill** pŏm (chún) mâi sa-bai
illegal pìt gòt-măi
illegible àhn mâi òrk
illness kwahm jèp bpòo-ay
imitation (*leather etc*) tee-um
immediately tun-tee
Immigration Department grom dtròo-ut kon kâo meu-ung
import (*verb*) num kâo
important sŭm-kun; **it's very important** sŭm-kun mâhk; **it's not important** mâi sŭm-kun
impossible bpen bpai mâi dâi
impressive nâh têung
improve: it's improving dee kêun; **I want to improve my Thai** pŏm (chún) yàhk ja pôot pah-săh tai hâi dee kêun
in: in my room nai hôrng pŏm (chún); **in the town centre** nai jai glahng meu-ung; **in London** nai

lorn-dorn; **in one hour's time** pai nai chôo-a mohng nèung; **in August** deu-un sĭng-hah-kom; **in English** bpen pah-săh ung-grìt; **in Thai** bpen pah-săh tai; **is he in?** káo yòo mái?
inch néw; *see page 113*
include roo-um; **is that included in the price?** roo-um yòo nai rah-kah rĕu bplào?
incompetent mâi mee kwahm săh-mâht
inconvenient mâi sa-dòo-uk
increase (*verb*) pêrm
incredible (*very good, amazing*) wí-sàyt
indecent yàhp lohn
independent (*adjective*) bpen ìt-sa-rá
India bpra-tâyt in-dee-a
Indian (*adjective*) kàirk; **an Indian/the Indians** kàirk
indicator (*on car*) fai lée-o
indigestion ah-hăhn mâi yôy
indoors kâhng nai
industry òot-săh-hà-gum
inefficient mâi mee bpra-sìt-ti-pâhp
infected ùk-sàyp
infection ah-gahn ùk-sàyp
infectious disease rôhk dùt dtòr
inflamed ùk-sàyp
inflation ngern fèr
informal (*clothes, occasion, meeting*) bpen gun ayng
information kào săhn
information desk têe sòrp tăhm
information office sŭm-núk ngahn kào săhn
injection: I had an injection pŏm (chún) chèet yah; **will I need an injection?** pŏm (chún) dtôrng chèet yah rĕu bplào?

injured bàht jèp; **she's been injured** káo bàht jèp
injury plǎir bàht jèp
innocent bor-ri-sòot
inquisitive yàhk róo yàhk hěn
insect ma-lairng
insect bite ma-lairng gùt
insecticide yah kâh ma-lairng
insect repellent yah gun ma-lairng
inside kâhng nai; **let's sit inside** bpai nûng kâhng nai tèr
insincere mâi jing jai
insist: I insist pǒm (chún) ka-yún ka-yor
insomnia norn mâi lùp
instant coffee gah-fair pǒng
instead tairn; **I'll have that one instead** kǒr ao un nún tairn; **instead of ...** tairn têe ja ...
insulating tape pâh táyp
insulin in-soo-lin
insult (noun) kum sòp bpra-màht
insurance bpra-gun; **write your company insurance here** kěe-un chêu bor-ri-sùt bpra-gun têe nêe
insurance policy ngêu-un kǎi bpra-gun
intellectual (noun) bpun-yah chon
intelligent cha-làht
intentional: it wasn't intentional mâi dâi dtûng jai
interest: places of interest sa-tǎhn têe nâh sǒn jai
interested: I'm very interested in ... pǒm (chún) sǒn jai ... mâhk
interesting nâh sǒn jai; **that's very interesting** nâh sǒn jai mâhk
international sǎh-gon
international driving licence/ driver's license bai kùp kèe sǎh-gon
interpret bplair; **would you interpret?** chôo-ay bplair hâi nòy dâi mái?
interpreter lâhm

intersection (crossroads) sèe yâirk
interval (during play etc) púk krêung
into nai; **I'm not into that** (don't like) pǒm (chún) mâi chôrp
introduce: may I introduce ...? pǒm (chún) kǒr náir-num hâi róo-jùk gùp ...
introvert kon ngêe-up
invalid kon pi-gahn
invalid chair gâo-êe mee lór sǔm-rùp kon pi-gahn
invitation bùt chern; **thank you for the invitation** kòrp-koon têe chern mah
invite chern choo-un; **I'd like to invite you out for a meal** pǒm (chún) yàhk ja choo-un koon bpai tahn ah-hǎhn dôo-ay gun
involved: I don't want to get involved in it pǒm (chún) mâi yàhk ja gèe-o kôrng
iodine ai-oh-deen
Ireland gòr ai-lairn
Irish ai-rít
iron (material) lèk; (for clothes) dtao rêet; **can you iron these for me?** chôo-ay rêet hâi nòy dâi mái?
ironmonger ráhn kǎi krêu-ung lèk
is bpen; see page 98
island gòr
isolated dòht-dèe-o
it mun; **it's my bag** (mun) bpen gra-bpǎo kǒrng pǒm (chún); **is it your car?** (mun) bpen rót kǒrng koon rěu bplào?; **it's expensive** (mun) pairng; **it's very tasty** (mun) a-ròy mâhk; **is it good?** (mun) dee mái?; **it's a long way** (mun) yòo glai; **where is it?** (mun) yòo têe nǎi?; **it's her** káo ayng; **it's me** pǒm (chún) ayng; **that's just it** (just the problem) nûn ná sêe; **that's it** (that's right) châi láir-o; see page 101
itch kun; **my arm itches** kun kǎirn
itinerary mǎi gum-nòt gahn

J

jack (*for car*) mâir rairng
jacket sêu-a nôrk
jam yairm; **a traffic jam** rót dùt; **I jammed on the brakes** pǒm (chún) yèe-up brayk
January mok-ga-rah-kom
Japan bpra-tâyt yêe-bpòon
Japanese (*adjective*) yêe-bpòon; **a Japanese/the Japanese** kon yêe-bpòon
jaundice rôhk dee-sâhn
jaw kǎh gun grai
jazz jáirt
jazz club jáirt klúp
jealous hěung; (*envious*) kêe ìt-chǎh
jeans yeen
jellyfish mairng ga-prOon
jetty tâh reu-a
Jew kon yew
jewel(le)ry pét ploy
Jewish yew
jiffy: **just a jiffy** děe-o
job ngahn; **just the job!** (*just right*) gum-lung dee; **it's a good job you told me!** dee têe kOon bòrk pǒm (chún)
jog: **I'm going for a jog** pǒm (chún) bpai jórk-gîng
jogging jórk-gîng
join: **I'd like to join** pǒm (chún) kǒr sa-mùk dôo-ay; **can I join you?** (*go with*) bpai dôo-ay kon dâi mái?; (*sit with*) kǒr nûng dôo-ay kon dâi mái?; **do you want to join us?** (*go with*) yàhk bpai dôo-ay gun mái?; (*sit with*) mah nûng dôo-ay gun mái?

joint (*in body*) kôr dtòr; (*to smoke*) gun-chah
joke (*verb*) pôot lên, dta-lòk; **you've got to be joking!** kOon nêe dta-lòk ná; **I was only joking** pǒm (chún) pôot lên tâo-nún; **it's no joke** mâi châi rêu-ung dta-lòk ná
jolly: **it was jolly good** dee mâhk; **jolly good!** dee mâhk!
journey gahn dern tahng; **safe journey!** kǒr hâi dern tahng doy-ee bplòrt-pai
jug yèu-uk; **a jug of water** yèu-uk náhm
July ga-rá-ga-dah-kom
jump: **you made me jump** tum hâi dtòk jai; **jump in!** (*to car*) kêun mah ray-o ray-o
jumper sêu-a sa-wét-dtêr
junction tahng yâirk
June mí-tOo-nah-yon
jungle bpàh; **in the jungle** nai bpàh
junk (*rubbish*) goh-roh-goh-sǒh; (*boat*) reu-a sǔm-pao
just: **just one** un dee-o tâo-nún; **just me** pǒm (chún) kon dee-o; **just for me** sǔm-rùp pǒm (chún) kon dee-o; **just a little** pee-ung dtàir nít-nòy tâo-nún; **just here** dtrong née; **not just now** mâi ao děe-o née; **that's just right** por dee láir-o; **it's just as good** dee tâo tâo gun; **he was here just now** pêrng hěn káo yòo mêu-a gêe née; **I've only just arrived** pǒm (chún) pêrng mah mêu-a gêe née ayng

K

kagul sêu-a nôrk
keen: I'm not keen pŏm (chún) mâi kôy chôrp
keep: can I keep it? pŏm (chún) gèp wái dâi mái?; **please keep it** ao wái ler-ee; **keep the change** mâi dtôrng torn; **will it keep?** (food) ja sĕe-a rĕu bplào?; **it's keeping me awake** mun tum hâi pŏm (chún) norn mâi lùp; **it keeps on breaking** dtàirk yòo rêu-ay ler-ee; **I can't keep anything down** (food) pŏm (chún) ah-jee-un bòy
kerb kòrp ta-nŏn
kerosene núm mun gáht
ketchup núm sórt ma-kĕu-a tâyt
kettle gah náhm
key goon-jair
kid: the kids pòo-uk dèk; **I'm not kidding** pŏm (chún) mâi pôot lên
kidneys (in body, food) tai
kill kâh
kilo gi-loh; see page 114
kilometre, kilometer gi-loh-mét; see page 113
kind: that's very kind koon jai dee mâhk; **this kind of ... ...** bàirp née

king nai lŏo-ung
kiosk dtôo
kiss (verb) jòop
kitchen hôrng kroo-a
kite wâo
Kleenex (tm) gra-dàht chét meu
knee hŏo-a kào
kneecap sa-bâh hŏo-a kào
knickers gahng gayng nai sa-dtree
knife mêet
knitting (act) gahn tùk mǎi prom; (material) mǎi prom
knitting needles mái tùk mǎi prom
knock: he's had a knock on the head hŏo-a káo tòok chon; **he's been knocked over** káo tòok rót chon
knot (in rope) bpom; **to tie a knot** pòok bpom
know (a person, place) róo-jùk; (a fact, something: informal word) róo; (formal word) sâhp; **I don't know** pŏm (chún) mâi róo/sâhp; **do you know a good restaurant?** koon róo-jùk ráhn ah-hǎhn dee dee mái?; **who knows?** krai ja róo?; **I didn't know that** pŏm (chún) mâi róo/sâhp mah gòrn; **I don't know him** pŏm (chún) mâi róo-jùk káo

L

label bpâi

Labour/Labor Department grom rairng ngahn

laces (*for shoes*) chêu-uk rorng táo

ladies (room) hôrng náhm pôo-yǐng

lady soo-pâhp sa-dtree; **ladies and gentlemen!** tûn soo-pâhp boo-ròot láir sa-dtree

lager bee-a

lake ta-lay sàhp

lamp kohm fai

lamppost sǎo fai fáh

lampshade póh fai

land (*not sea*) din; **when does the plane land?** krêu-ung bin long mêu-a rài?

landlord jâo kǒrng bâhn

landscape poo-mi-bpra-tâyt

lane (*on motorway*) chôrng; (*narrow street*) soy

language pah-sǎh

language course bàirp ree-un pah-sǎh

Lao (*adjective*) lao; **a Lao/the Laos** kon lao

Laos bpra-tâyt lao

large yài

laryngitis rôhk chôrng kor ùk-sàyp

last (*previous*) têe láir-o; (*final*) sòot-tái; **last year** bpee têe láir-o; **last Wednesday** wun póot têe láir-o; **last night** mêu-a keun née; **when's the last bus?** rót-may têe-o sòot-tái òrk gèe mohng?; **one last drink** dèum gâir-o sòot-tái; **when were you last in London?** mah lorn-dorn krúng lǔng sòot mêu-a rài?; **at last!** nai têe sòot!; **how long does it last?** chái way-lah nahn tâo-rài?

last name nahm sa⸱⸱oon

late (*in the morning*) sǎi; (*at night*) dèuk; (*behind schedule*) cháh; **sorry I'm late** kǒr-tôht têe mah cháh; **don't be late** yàh mah cháh; **the bus was late** (*leaving*) rót òrk cháh; (*arriving*) rót mah těung cháh; **we'll be back late tonight** rao ja glùp mah dèuk; **it's getting late** dèuk láir-o; **is it that late!** cháh yung ngún chee-o lěr; **it's too late now** cháh bpai láir-o; **I'm a late riser** rǒm (chún) bpen kon dtèun sǎi

lately mêu-a ray-o ray-o née

later tee lǔng; **later on** tee lǔng; **I'll come back later** děe-o ja glùp mah; **see you later** děe-o jer gun èek; **no later than Tuesday** mâi cháh bpai gwàh wun ung-kahn

latest: the latest news kào lâh sòot; **at the latest** yàhng cháh têe sòot

laugh hǒo-a rór; **don't laugh** yàh hǒo-a rór ná; **it's no laughing matter** mâi châi rêu-ung hǒo-a rór lên

launder súk rêet; **can you launder these for me?** chôo-ay súk rêet hâi nòy, dâi mái?

laundry (*place*) ráhn súk sêu-a pâh; **could you get the laundry done?** chôo-ay súk rêet sêu-a pâh hâi nòy, dâi mái?

laundryman, laundrywoman kon súk pâh

lavatory hôrng náhm

law gòt-mǎi; **against the law** pìt gòt-mǎi

lawn sa-nǎhm yâh

lawyer ta-nai kwahm

laxative yah tài

lay-by têe púk jòrt kâhng tahng

lazy kêe gèe-ut; **don't be lazy** yàh kêe gèe-ut; **a nice lazy holiday** way-lah yòot púk pòrn dtahm sa-bai

lead (*electrical*) săi fai fáh; **where does this road lead?** ta-nǒn săi née bpai nǎi?

leaf bai mái

leaflet àyk-ga-sǎhn; **do you have any leaflets on ...?** mee àyk-ga-sǎhn rêu-ung ... mái?

leak rôo-a; **the roof leaks** lǔng-kah rôo-a

learn: I want to learn ... pǒm (chún) yàhk ja ree-un ...

learner: I'm just a learner pǒm (chún) bpen kon gum-lung hùt ree-un

lease (*verb*) hâi châo

least: not in the least mâi ler-ee; **at least 50** yàhng nóy hâa sìp

leather nǔng

leave: when does the bus leave? rót-may òrk gèe mohng?; **I leave tomorrow** pǒm (chún) ja bpai prôong née; **he left this morning** káo bpai mêu-a cháo née; **may I leave this here?** kǒr fàhk wái têe nêe dâi mái?; **I left my bag in the bar** pǒm (chún) tíng gra-bpǎo wái têe bah; **she left her bag here** káo tíng gra-bpǎo wái têe nêe; **leave the window open please** chôo-ay bpèrt nâh-dtàhng tíng wái; **there's not much left** mâi kôy mee lěu-a yòo; **I've hardly any money left** pǒm (chún) mâi kôy mee ngern lěu-a yòo; **I'll leave it up to you** láir-o dtàir koon

left sái; **on the left** tahng sái

left-hand drive poo-ung mah-lai sái

left-handed ta-nùt meu sái

left luggage office têe fàhk gra-bpǎo

leg kǎh

legal tòok gòt-mǎi

legal aid kwahm chôo-ay lěu-a tahng gòt-mǎi

lemon ma-nao

lemonade núm ma-nao

lemon tea chah sài ma-nao

lend: would you lend me your ...? kǒr yeum ... nòy, dâi mái?

lens (*of camera*) layn glôrng; (*contact*) korn-táirk layn

lens cap fǎh layn

lesbian 'lesbian'

less: less than an hour mâi těung chôo-a mohng; **less than that** nóy gwàh nún; **less hot** rórn nóy gwàh

lesson bòt ree-un; **do you give lessons?** rúp sǒrn mái?

let: would you let me use it? kǒr chái nòy dâi mái?; **will you let me know?** chôo-ay bòrk hâi pǒm (chún) sâhp dôo-ay; **I'll let you know** pǒm (chún) ja bòrk hâi sâhp; **let me try** kǒr lorng doo nòy, dâi mái?; **let me go!** bplòy ná!; **let's leave now** bpai gun tèr; **let's not go yet** yàh pêrng bpai ler-ee; **will you let me off at ...?** kǒr long têe ... dâi mái?; **rooms to let** hôrng hâi châo

letter (*in mail*) jòt-mǎi; (*of alphabet*) dtoo-a ùk-sǒrn; **are there any letters for me?** mee jòt-mǎi mah těung pǒm (chún) mái?

letterbox dtôo jòt-mǎi

lettuce pùk-gàht

level crossing tahng rót fai pàhn

lever (*noun*) kun yôhk

liable (*responsible*) rúp pìt chôrp

liberated: a liberated woman pôo-yǐng sa-mǎi mài

library hôrng sa-mòot

licence, license (*driving*) bai kùp kèe

license plate (*on car*) bpâi ta-bee-un rót

lid fǎh

lie (*tell untruth*) goh-hòk; **can he lie down for a while?** norn long děe-o dâi mái?; **I want to go and lie down** pǒm (chún) yàhk ja bpai norn púk

lie-in: I'm going to have a lie-in tomorrow prôong née pǒm (chún) ja norn púk

life chee-wít; **not on your life!** mâi mee wun!; **that's life!** nêe lâ chee-wít!

lifebelt choo chêep
lifeboat reu-a choo chêep
life insurance bpra-gun chee-wít
life jacket sêu-a choo chêep
lift (*in hotel etc*) líf; **could you give me a lift?** chôo-ay bpai sòng nòy, dâi mái?; **do you want a lift?** bpai sòng hâi ao mái?; **thanks for the lift** kòrp-koon têe mah sòng; **I got a lift** mee kon mah sòng
light (*noun*) fai; (*not heavy*) bao; **the light was on** fai bpèrt yòo; **do you have a light?** (*for cigarette*) mee mái kèet mái?; **a light meal** ah-hǎhn bao bao; **light blue** sěe fáh
light bulb lòrt fai fáh
lighter (*cigarette*) fai cháirk
lighthouse gra-johm fai
light meter krêu-ung wút fai fáh
lightning fáh lâirp
like: I'd like a ... pǒm (chún) ao ...; **I'd like to ...** pǒm (chán) yàhk ja ...; **would you like a ...?** koon ao ... mái?; **would you like to come too?** koon yàhk ja mah dôo-ay mái?; **I'd like to** yàhk; **I like it** pǒm (chún) chôrp; **I like you** pǒm (chún) chôrp koon; **I don't like it** pǒm (chún) mâi chôrp; **he doesn't like it** káo mâi chôrp; **do you like ...?** koon chôrp ...?; **I like swimming** pǒm (chún) chôrp wâi náhm; **OK, if you like** dtòk long dtahm jai koon; **what's it like?** bpen yung ngai?; **do it like this** tum yung ngée ná; **one like that** měu-un un nún
lilo dtee-ung lom
line (*on paper*) sên; (*telephone*) sǎi; (*of people*) tǎir-o; **would you give me a line?** (*telephone*) chôo-ay dtòr sǎi hâi nòy
linen (*for beds*) pâh bpoo têe norn
linguist kon gèng pah-sǎh; **I'm no linguist** pǒm (chún) mâi gèng pah-sǎh
lining súp nai
lip rim fěe bpàhk
lipstick líp sa-dtík
liquor lâo

liquor store ráhn kǎi lâo
list (*of things*) rai gahn; (*of names*) rai chêu
listen: I'd like to listen to ... pǒm (chún) yàhk ja fung ...; **listen!** fung si!
litre, liter lít; *see page 114*
litter (*rubbish*) ka-yà
little lék; **just a little, thanks** nít dee-o tâo-nún; **just a very little** pee-ung dtàir nít dee-o tâo-nún; **a little cream** kreem sùk nít nèung; **a little more** èek nít nèung; **a little better** kôy yung chôo-a nòy; **that's too little** (*not enough*) mâi por
live yòo; **I live in ...** pǒm (chún) yòo têe ...; **where do you live?** koon yòo têe nǎi?; **where does he live?** káo yòo têe nǎi?; **we live together** rao yòo dôo-ay gun
lively (*person, town*) mee chee-wít chee-wah
liver (*in body, food*) dtùp
lizard jîng-jòk
loaf bporn
lobby (*of hotel*) pa-nàirk dtôrn rúp
lobster gôong yài
local: a local dish ah-hǎhn péun meu-ung; **a local newspaper** núng sěu pim tórng tìn
lock (*noun*) goon-jair; **it's locked** sài goon-jair láir-o; **I locked myself out of my room** bpìt goon-jair láir-o kâo hôrng mâi dâi
locker (*for luggage etc*) dtôo gèp gra-bpǎo
log: I slept like a log pǒm (chún) norn lùp sa-nìt
lollipop om-yím
London lorn-dorn
lonely ngǎo; **are you lonely?** koon ngǎo mái?
long yao; **how long does it take?** chái way-lah nahn tâo-rài?; **is it a long way?** yòo glai mái?; **a long time** nahn; **I won't be long** děe-o děe-o; **don't be long** yàh hâi nahn ná; **that was long ago** nahn mah láir-o; **I'd like to stay longer** pǒm (chún) yàhk

ja yòo dtòr èek; **long time no see!**
mâi dâi póp sěe-a dtûng nahn; **so
long!** chôhk dee ná
long distance call toh tahng glai
loo: where's the loo? hôrng náhm
yòo têe nǎi?; **I want to go to the loo**
pǒm (chún) dtôrng bpai hôrng
náhm
look: that looks good tâh tahng dee;
you look tired koon tâh tahng nèu-
ay; **I'm just looking, thanks** pǒm
(chún) chom doo tâo-nún; **you don't
look your age** koon nâh òrn gwàh
ah-yóo; **look at him** doo káo si; **I'm
looking for ...** pǒm (chún) gum-lung
hǎh ...; **look out!** ra-wung ná!; **can I
have a look?** kǒr doo nòy, dâi mái?;
can I have a look around? kǒr doo
nòy, dâi mái?
loose (*button, handle etc*) lòot; (*fit*) lǒo-
um
loose change sàyt sa-dtung
lorry rót bun-tòok
lorry driver kon kùp rót bun-tóok
lose: I've lost my ... ... kǒrng pǒm
(chún) hǎi; **I'm lost** pǒm (chún)
lǒng tahng
lot: a lot, lots mâhk; **not a lot** mâi
mâhk; **a lot of money** ngern mâhk;
a lot of women pôo-yǐng mâhk; **a
lot cooler** yen gwàh mâhk; **I like it
a lot** pǒm (chún) chôrp mâhk; **is it
a lot further?** èek glai mâhk mái?;
I'll take the (whole) lot pǒm (chún)

ao bpai túng mòt
lotion yah tah
lottery lórt-dter-rêe
loud dung; **the music is rather loud**
don-dtree dung bpai nòy
lounge (*in house, hotel*) hôrng tǒhng
lousy (*meal, hotel, holiday,* weather)
mâi ao nǎi
love: I love you pǒm (chún) rúk ter;
he's fallen in love káo lǒng rúk
láir-o; **I love Thailand** pǒm (chún)
rúk meu-ung tai
lovely (*meal, view, weather, present etc*)
yêe-um ler-ee
low (*prices, bridge*) dtùm
**lower: can you lower the price a
little?** lót rah-kah nòy, dâi mái?
low beam fai dtùm
LP pàirn sěe-ung L.P.
luck chôhk; **hard luck!** chôhk rái!;
good luck! chôhk dee!; **just my
luck!** (*I always have bad luck*) soo-ay
jing jing ná!; **it was pure luck** flóok
jing jing ler-ee
lucky: that's lucky! chôhk dee táir!
lucky charm krêu-ung chôhk krêu-
ung lahng
luggage gra-bpǎo
lumbago rôhk bpòo-ut sa-ay-o
lump (*medical*) néu-a ngôrk
lunch ah-hǎhn glahng wun
lungs bpòrt
luxurious (*hotel, furnishings*) rǒo-rǎh
luxury kǒrng fôom feu-ay

M

mad bâh
magazine nít-ta-ya-sǎhn
magnificent (*view*) sǒo-ay mâhk; (*day*)
ah-gàht dee mâhk; (*meal*) a-ròy
mâhk
maid (*chambermaid*) yǐng rúp chái

maiden name nahm sa-goon derm
mail jòt-mǎi; **is there any mail for
me?** mee jòt-mǎi sǔm-rùp pǒm
(chún) mái?
mailbox dtôo bprai-sa-nee
main sǔm-kun; **the main reason**

hàyt-pǒn sǔm-kun; **where's the main post office?** bprai-sa-nee glahng yòo têe nǎi?

main road (*in town, in country*) ta-nǒn yài

make tum; **do you make them yourself?** tum ayng rěu?; **it's very well made** tum dee mâhk; **what does that make altogether?** túng mòt tâo-rài?; **I make it only 500 baht** pǒm (chún) kít wâh hâh róy bàht tâo-nún

make-up krêu-ung sǔm-ahng

make-up remover yah láhng

malaria kâi jùp sùn

man pôo-chai

manager pôo-jùt-gahn; **may I see the manager?** kǒr póp pôo-jùt-gahn nòy

mango ma-môo-ung

manicure tum lép

mangosteen mung-kóot

many mâhk

map: a map of ... pǎirn-têe ...; **it's not on this map** mâi mee yòo nai pǎirn-têe née

March mee-nah-kom

marijuana gun-chah

mark: there's a mark on it mee dtum-nì; **could you mark it on the map for me?** tum krêu-ung mǎi bon pǎirn-têe hâi nòy, dâi mái?

market (*noun*) dta-làht; **floating market** dta-làht náhm

marmalade yairm

married: are you married? koon dtàirng ngahn láir-o rěu yung?; **I'm married** pǒm (chún) dtàirng ngahn láir-o

mascara mair-sa-kah-rah

mass: I'd like to go to mass yàhk bpai bòht

massage nôo-ut

mast sǎo

matches mái kèet

material (*cloth*) pâh

matter: it doesn't matter mâi bpen rai; **what's the matter?** (*with you*) bpen a-rai?; (*what's going on*) rêu-ung a-rai gun?

mattress têe norn

maximum (*noun*) kèet sǒong sòot

May préut-sa-pah-kom

may: may I ...? pǒm (chún) ... dâi mái?; **may I smoke?** pǒm (chún) sòop boo-rèe nòy, dâi mái?; **may I have another bottle?** kǒr èek kòo-ut nèung; **may I have a look?** kǒr doo nòy, dâi mái?

maybe bahng tee; **maybe not** bahng tee mâi

mayonnaise náhm sa-lùt

me (*male speaker*) pǒm; (*female speaker*) chún; **come with me** mah gùp pǒm (chún); **it's for me** sǔm-rùp pǒm (chún); **it's me** pǒm (chún) ayng; **me too** pǒm (chún) gôr měu-un gun; *see page 101*

meal: that was an excellent meal ah-hǎhn a-ròy mâhk; **does that include meals?** rôo-um túng ah-hǎhn dôo-ay rěu bplào?

mean: what does this word mean? kum née bplàir wâh a-rai?; **what does he mean?** káo mǎi kwahm wâh a-rai?

measles rôhk hùt; **German measles** rôhk hùt yer-ra-mun

measurements ka-nàht

meat néu-a

mechanic: do you have a mechanic here? têe nêe mee châhng krêu-ung mái?

medicine yah

medium (*adjective*) glahng

medium-rare sòok sòok dìp dìp

medium-sized ka-nàht glahng

meet: pleased to meet you yin dee têe róo-jùk gun; **where shall we meet?** póp gun têe nǎi?; **let's meet up again** póp gun mài ná

meeting (*formal meeting, conference*) bpra-choom

meeting place têe nút póp

Mekhong (*tm: whisky*) mâir-kǒhng; (*river*) mâir-náhm kǒhng

melon: water melon dtairng moh; **musk melon** dtairng tai

member sa-mah-chík; **I'd like to**

become a member pǒm (chún) yàhk
bpen sa-mah-chík
men pôo-chai
mend: can you mend this? koon
sôrm un née dâi mái?
mendicant monk pra-tóo-dong
men's room hôrng náhm pôo-chai
mention: don't mention it mâi bpen
rai
menu may-noo; rai-gahn ah-hǎhn;
may I have the menu please? kǒr
may-noo nòy krúp (kâ)
merchant (male) pôr káh; (female)
mâir káh
merit: to make merit tum boon
('making merit' refers to the act of
performing good deeds, such as offering
food to monks, which is supposed to
bring merit to the donor and to ensure a
better re-birth in subsequent lives)
mess: it's a mess (untidy, dirty) lér-tér;
(situation) yôong bpai mòt
message: are there any messages for
me? mee krai sùng a-rai wái rěu
bplào?; I'd like to leave a message
for ... pǒm (chún) yàhk ja fàhk bòrk
a-rai hâi ...
metal (noun) loh-hà
metre, meter máyt, see page 113
midday: at midday tee-ung wun
middle: in the middle yòo dtrong
glahng; in the middle of the road
glahng ta-nǒn
midnight: at midnight tee-ung keun
might: I might want to stay another
3 days bahng tee pǒm (chún) àht ja
yòo èek sǎhm wun; you might have
warned me! tum-mai mâi bòrk pǒm
(chún) gòrn?
migraine bpòo-ut hǒo-a kâhng dee-o
mild (taste) mâi pèt
mile mai; that's miles away! yòo glai
mâhk!; see page 113
mileometer krêu-ung bòrk rá-yá
tahng
military (noun) gahn ta-hǎhn
milk nom
milkshake 'milkshake'
millimetre, millimeter min-li-máyt

minced meat néu-a sùp
mind: I don't mind (it doesn't matter)
mâi bpen rai; (it's up to you) láir-o
dtàir; would you mind if I ...? kǒr
... nòy, dâi mái?; never mind mâi
bpen rai; I've changed my mind
pǒm (chún) bplèe-un jai láir-o
mine: it's mine kǒrng pǒm (chún);
see page 102
mineral water núm râe
minimum (adjective) nóy tee sòot
minus lóp
minute nah-tee; in a minute èek
bpra-dǐe-o; just a minute dǐe-o,
dǐe-o
mirror gra-jòk ngao
Miss nahng-sǎo
miss: I miss you pǒm (chún) kít
těung koon; there's a ... missing
mee ... hǎi bpai; we missed the bus
rao dtòk rót-may
mist mòrk
mistake kwahm pìt; I think there's a
mistake here pǒm (chún) kít wâh
mee kôr pìt lék nòy
misunderstanding kwahm kâo jai pìt
mixture sòo-un pa-sǒm
mix-up: there's been some sort of
mix-up with ... pǒm (chún) róo-sèuk
wâh mee kwahm kâo jai pìt gèe-o
gùp ...
modern tun-sa-mǎi
modern art sǐn-la-bpà sa-mǎi mài
moisturizer kreem bum-roong pěw
moment: I won't be a moment ror
dǐe-o
monastery wút
Monday wun jun
money ngern; (informal word) sa-
dtung; I don't have any money pǒm
(chún) mâi mee sa-dtung; do you
take English/American money? rúp
ngern ung-grìt/a-may-ri-gun rěu
bplào krúp (kâ)?
monk prá
monsoon mor-ra-sǒom
month deu-un
monument a-nóo-sǎh-wa-ree
moon prá jun

moorings tâh reu-a
moped rót mor-dter-sai
more èek, gwàh; **may I have some
more?** kǒr èek nòy krúp (kâ); **more
water, please** kǒr náhm èek nòy
krúp (kâ); **no more, thanks** por
láir-o, kòrp-koon krúp (kâ); **more
expensive** pairng gwàh; **more than
50** hâh sìp gwàh; **more than that**
mâhk gwàh nún; **a lot more** èek
mâhk; **I don't stay there any more**
pǒm (chún) mâi dâi yòo têe nûn èek
láir-o
morning cháo; **good morning** sa-
wùt-dee krúp (kâ); **this morning**
cháo née; **in the morning** dtorn
cháo
mosquito yoong
mosquito net móong
most: I like this one most pǒm
(chún) chôrp un née mâhk têe sòot;
most of the time way-lah sòo-un
mâhk; **most hotels** rohng-rairm
sòo-un mâhk
mother: my mother mâir kǒrng pǒm
(chún)
motif (*in pattern*) lai
motor krêu-ung yon
motorbike rót mor-dter-sai
motorboat reu-a yon
motorist kon kùp rót
motorway tahng dòo-un
mountain poo-kǎo; **up in the
mountains** yòo bon poo-kǎo; **a
mountain village** mòo-bâhn bon
poo-kǎo
mouse nǒo
moustache nòo-ut
mouth bpàhk
move: he's moved to another hotel
káo yái bpai yòo èek rohng-rairm

nèung; **could you move your car?**
chôo-ay lêu-un rót kǒrng koon, dâi
mái?
movie nǔng; **let's go to the movies**
bpai doo nǔng dôo-ay gun mái?
movie camera glôrng tài nǔng
movie theater rohng-nǔng
Mr nai
Mrs nahng
Ms *no Thai equivalent*
much mâhk; **much better** dee kêun
mâhk; **much cooler** yen long mâhk;
not much mâi mâhk; **not so much**
mâi mâhk tâo-rài
mud klohn
muffler (*on car*) tôr ai-sǐa
mug: I've been mugged pǒm (chún)
tòok jêe
muggy (*weather*) ah-gàht òp-âo
mumps kahng toom
murals jìt-dta-gum fǎh pa-nǔng
muscle glâhm néu-a
museum pí-pít-ta-pun
mushroom hèt
music don-dtree; **guitar music** don-
dtree gee-dtah; **do you have the
sheet music for ...?** mee nóht don-
dtree sǔm-rùp ...? mái?
musician núk don-dtree
mussels hǒy mairng pôo
must: I must ... pǒm (chún) dtôrng
...; **I mustn't drink alcohol** pǒm
(chún) dtôrng mâi gin lâo; **you
mustn't forget** yàh leum ná
mustache nòo-ut
mustard núm jîm mut-sa-dtàht
my kǒrng pǒm (chún); **my room**
hôrng kǒrng pǒm (chún); *see page
100*
myself: I'll do it myself pǒm (chún)
ja tum ayng

N

nail (*of finger*) lép meu; (*in wood*) dtah-bpoo
nail clippers têe dtùt lép
nailfile dta-bai fŏn lép
nail polish yah tah lép
nail polish remover núm yah láhng lép
nail scissors dta-grai dtùt lép
naked bpleu-ay
name (*first name*) chêu; (*nickname*) chêu lên; (*surname*) nahm sa-gOOn; **what's your name?** kOOn chêu a-rai?; **what's its name?** rêe-uk wâh a-rai?; **my name is ...** pŏm (chún) chêu ...; *see page 110*
nap: he's having a nap káo ngêep
napkin (*serviette*) pâh chét meu
nappy pâh ôrm
nappy-liners pâh rorng pâh ôrm
narrow (*road*) kâirp
narrow-minded jai kâirp
nasty (*taste, person, weather*) nâh tOO-râyt; (*cut*) plăir wèr
national hàirng châht
nationality sŭn-châht
National Museum pí-pít-ta-pun hàirng châht
National Stadium sa-năhm gee-lah hàirng châht
natural tum-ma-châht
naturally (*in a natural way*) dtahm tum-ma-châht; (*of course*) nâir-norn
nature (*trees etc*) tum-ma-châht
nausea ah-gahn klêun hĕe-un
near glâi; **is it near here?** yòo glâi mái?; **near the window** glâi náh-dtàhng; **do you go near ...?** kOOn pàhn bpai glâi glâi ... mái?; **where is the nearest ...?** ... glâi têe sòot yòo têe năi?

nearby yòo glâi
nearly gèu-up
neat (*room etc*) rêe-up róy; (*drink*) mâi dterm náhm
necessary jum-bpen; **is it necessary to ...?** jum-bpen dtôrng ... rĕu bplào?; **it's not necessary** mâi jum-bpen
neck (*of body, of dress, shirt*) kor
necklace sôy kor
necktie nék tai
need: I need a ... pŏm (chún) dtôrng-gahn ...; **do I need a ...?** pŏm (chún) dtôrng-gahn ... rĕu bplào?; **it needs more salt** dtôrng sài gleu-a èek nòy; **there's no need** mâi dtôrng; **there's no need to shout!** mâi jum-bpen dtôrng dta-gohn!
needle kĕm
negative (*film*) feem
neighbo(u)r pêu-un bâhn
neighbo(u)rhood yâhn
neither: he's not going — neither am I káo mâi bpai — pŏm (chún) gôr mâi bpai mĕu-un gun; **would you like coke or beer? — neither** kOOn ao koh-lâh réu bee-a? — mâi ao túng sŏrng yàhng
nephew: my nephew lăhn chai
nervous bpòrt
net (*mosquito*) móong; (*tennis*) dtah-kài; (*fishing*) hăir
neurotic bpra-sàht
neutral (*country*) bpen glahng; (*gear*) gee-a wâhng
never mâi ker-ee; **I've never been there** pŏm (chún) mâi ker-ee bpai
new mài
news kào; **is there any news?** mee kào a-rai mái?

newspaper núng-sěu pim; **do you have any English newspapers?** mee núng-sěu pim ung-grìt mái?; **do you have any English language newspapers?** mee núng-sěu pim pah-săh ung-grìt mái?

newsstand dtôo núng-sěu pim

New Year bpee mài; **Happy New Year** sa-wùt dee bpee mài; **Chinese New Year** dtròot jeen; **Thai New Year** sŏng-grahn

New Year's Eve wun sîn bpee

New York new yórk

New Zealand bpra-tâyt new see-láirn

New Zealander kon new see-láirn

next nâh; **next to** dtìt gùp; **it's at the next intersection** yòo yâirk nâh; **next week/Monday** ah-tít/wun jun nâh; **next to the post office** dtìt gùp bprai-sa-nee; **the one next to that** dtìt gùp un nún

nextdoor (adverb, adjective) bâhn tùt bpai

next of kin yâht

nice (person, weather) dee; (meal) a-ròy; (town) sŏo-ay; **that's very nice of you** koon jai dee mâhk; **a nice cold drink** krêu-ung dèum yen yen

nickname chêu-lên

niece: my niece lăhn săo

night glahng keun; **for one night** keun dee-o; **for three nights** săhm keun; **good night** sa-wùt dee; **at night** dtorn glahng keun

nightcap (drink) gâir-o sòot tái

nightclub náit klúp

nightdress chóot norn

night flight têe-o bin glahng keun

nightie chóot norn

night-life chee-wít glahng keun

nightmare fŭn rái

night watchman yahm

nits (bugs, in hair) kài hăo

no mâi; **I've no money** pŏm (chún) mâi mee ngern; **there's no more** mâi mee lěu-a yòo; **no more than ...** mâi mâhk gwàh ...; **oh no!** (upset) dtai jing!; **no smoking** hâhm sòop boo-rèe; see page 105

nobody mâi mee krai

noise sěe-ung

noisy nòo-uk hŏo; **it's too noisy** nòo-uk hŏo gern bpai

non-alcoholic (drink) náhm kòo-ut

nonsense mâi bpen rêu-ung

non-smoking (compartment, section of plane) hâhm sòop boo-rèe

non-stop (travel) mâi yòot

noodles (general term) gŏo-ay dtěe-o; **egg noodles** ba-mèe; **fried noodles** (Thai-style) pùt tai; **fried noodles** (Chinese-style) pùt see éw

noodle shop ráhn gŏo-ay dtěe-o

no-one mâi mee krai

nor: she doesn't want to stay here — nor do I káo mâi yàhk ja púk yòo têe nêe — pŏm (chún) gôr mâi yàhk měu-un gun; **nor me** pŏm (chún) gôr mâi měu-un gun

normal tum-ma-dah

north něu-a; **to the north** tahng něu-a

northeast dta-wun òrk chěe-ung něu-a; **to the northeast** tít dta-wun òrk chěe-ung něu-a

north-eastern: the north-eastern region of Thailand pâhk ee-săhn

northern: the northern region of Thailand pâhk něu-a

Northern Ireland ai-lairn něu-a

North Vietnam wêe-ut nahm něu-a

northwest dta-wun dtòk chěe-ung něu-a; **to the northwest** tít dta-wun dtòk chěe-ung něu-a

nose ja-mòok; **my nose is bleeding** lêu-ut gum-dao lăi

not mâi; **I don't smoke** pŏm (chún) mâi sòop; **he didn't say anything** káo mâi dâi pôot a-rai; **it's not important** mâi sŭm-kun; **not that one** mâi châi un nún; **not for me** mâi châi sŭm-rùp pŏm (chún); see page 108

note (bank note) bai báirng; (written message etc) bun-téuk

notebook sa-mòot

nothing mâi mee a-rai

November deu-un préut-sa-jìk-gah-

yon
now (*at this moment*) dĕe-o née; (*nowa-days*) bpùt-joo-bun-née; **not now** mâi châi dĕe-o née
nowhere: I have nowhere to stay pŏm (chún) mâi mee têe púk; **there's nowhere to park** mâi mee têe jòrt
nuisance: he's being a nuisance (*pestering woman etc*) káo yôong
numb (*limb etc*) chah

number (*figure*) mǎi lâyk; **(house) number** 27 bâhn lâyk têe yêe sìp jèt; **telephone number** ber toh-ra-sùp; **what number?** ber a-rai?
number plates bpâi ta-bee-un rót
nurse nahng pa-yah-bahn
nursery (*at airport etc, for children*) sa-tǎhn lée-ung dèk lék
nut (*food*) tòo-a; (*for bolt*) nórt
nutter: he's a nutter (*is crazy*) káo bpra-sàht

O

oar mái pai
obligatory bung-kúp
oblige: much obliged (*thank you*) kòrp-koon mâhk
obnoxious (*person*) nâh yàhp kai
obvious: that's obvious hĕn chút chút
occasionally bahng krúng bahng krao
o'clock *see page 111*
October deu-un dtoo-lah
octopus bplah-mèuk yúk
odd (*strange*) bplàirk; (*number*) lâyk kêe
odometer krêu-ung bòrk rá-yá tahng
of kŏrng; **the name of the hotel** chêu kŏrng rohng rairm; **have one of mine** ao kŏrng pŏm (chún) sée
off: 20% off lót yêe sìp bper-sen; **the lights were off** fai bpìt láir-o; **just off the main road** yâirk ta-nŏn yài bpai nòy
offend: don't be offended yàh gròht ná
office (*place of work*) têe tum ngahn
officer (*said to policeman*) nai dtum-ròo-ut
official (*noun*) jâo nâh-têe; **is that official?** bpen tahng-gahn mái?
off-season mâi châi nâh

often bòy bòy; **not often** mâi bòy
oil (*motor oil*) núm mun krêu-ung; (*vegetable oil*) núm mun pêut; **it's losing oil** núm mun rôo-a; **will you change the oil?** chôo-ay bplèe-un núm mun krêu-ung nòy, dâi mái?; **the oil light's flashing** fai núm mun krêu-ung ga-príp yòo
oil painting pâhp sĕe núm mun
oil pressure kwahm gòt mun krêu-ung
ointment yah tah
OK oh-kay; **are you OK?** koon oh-kay mái?; **that's OK thanks** oh-kay kòrp-koon; **that's OK by me** pŏm (chún) oh-kay láir-o
old (*things*) gào; (*people*) gàir; **how old are you?** koon ah-yóo tâo-rài?
old-fashioned láh sa-mǎi
old town (*old part of town*) meu-ung gào
olive ma-gòrk
olive oil núm mun ma-gòrk
omelet(t)e kài jee-o
on bon; **on the roof** bon lŭng-kah; **on the beach** chai ta-lay; **on Friday** wun sòok; **on television** nai tee wee; **I don't have it on me** pŏm (chún) mâi dâi ao mah dôo-ay; **this drink's on**

me lâw nêe pǒm (chún) lée-ung; **a
book on Thailand** núng-sěu gèe-o
gùp meu-ung tai; **the warning light
comes on** fai dteu-un bpèrt láir-o;
the light was on fai bpèrt yòo láir-o;
what's on in town? nai meu-ung
mee a-rai doo bâhng?; **it's just not
on!** (*not acceptable*) bpen bpai mâi
dâi

once (*one time*) krúng nèung; (*formerly*)
mêu-a gòrn née; **at once**
(*immediately*) tun-tee

one nèung; **that one** un nún; **the
green one** un sěe kěe-o; **the one
with the black skirt on** kon sài gra-
bprohng sěe dum; **the one in the
blue shirt** kon sài sêu-a sěe fáh

onion hǒo-a hǒrm

only tâo-nún; **only one** un dee-o tâo-
nún; **only once** krúng dee-o tâo-
nún; **it's only 9 o'clock** pêung gâo
mohng tâo-nún; **I've only just
arrived** pǒm (chún) pêung mah
děe-o née ayng

open (*adjective*) bpèrt; **when do you
open?** bpèrt gèe mohng?; **in the
open** (*in open air*) glahng jâirng; **it
won't open** bpèrt mâi dâi

opening times way-lah bpìt-bpèrt

open top (*car*) bpèrt bpa-toon

operation (*medical*) gahn pàh dtùt

operator (*telephone*) pa-núk ngahn
toh-ra-sùp

opportunity oh-gàht; **I don't get any
opportunity** pǒm (chún) mâi mee
oh-gàht

opposite: opposite the temple dtrong
kâhm wút; **it's directly opposite** yòo
dtrong kâhm

oppressive (*heat*) èut-ùt

optician jùk-sòo pâirt

optimistic morng lôhk nai ngâir dee

option tahng lêu-uk; **an optional
excursion** mee rai-gahn têe-o hâi
lêu-uk

or rěu

orange (*fruit*) sôm; (*colour*) sěe sôm

orange juice (*fresh, frizzy, diluted*)
núm sôm

orchestra wong don-dtree

order: could we order now? (*in
restaurant*) kǒr sùng děe-o née dâi
mái?; **I've already ordered** pǒm
(chún) sùng láir-o; **I didn't order
that** pǒm (chún) mâi dâi sùng; **it's
out of order** (*lift etc*) sěe-a

ordinary tum-ma-dah

organization (*company*) ong-gahn

organize jùt gahn; **could you
organize it?** koon jùt gahn hâi nòy
dâi mái?

original táir; **is it an original?** bpen
kǒrng táir mái?

ornament krêu-ung bpra-dùp

ostentatious (*clothes, colour etc*) rǒo-
rǎh

other èun; **the other ...** èek ... nèung;
the other one (*person*) èek kon
nèung; (*thing*) èek un nèung; **the
other waiter** kon sérp èek kon
nèung; **other people** kon èun; **do
you have any others?** mee yàhng
èun mái?; **some other time, thanks**
ao wái wun lǔng!

otherwise mí-cha-nún

ouch! ôoy-ee!

ought: he ought to be here soon káo
nâh ja mah ray-o ray-o

ounce *see page 114*

our: our hotel rohng rairm kǒrng
rao; **our suitcases** agra-bpǎo kǒrng
rao; *see page 100*

ours kǒrng rao; **that's ours** nûn
kǒrng rao; *see page 102*

out: he's out káo mâi yòo; **get out!**
òrk bpai hâi pón!; **I'm out of money**
pǒm (chún) mòt ngern; **a few kilometres out of town** nôrk meu-ung
bpai jàrng sǎhm gi-loh

outboard (*motor*) krêu-ung reu-a

outdoors glahng jâirng

outlet bplúk fai

outside kâhng nôrk; **can we sit outside?** nûng kâhng nôrk dâi mái?

outskirts: on the outskirts of ...
chahn meu-ung ...

oven dtao òp

over: over here têe nêe; **over there**

têe nôhn; **over 100** róy gwàh; **I'm
burnt all over** pǒm (chún) mâi bpai
túng dtoo-a; **the holiday's over** wun
yòot mòt láir-o
overcharge: you've overcharged me
koon kít ngern mâhk bpai
overcoat sêu-a nôrk
overcooked sòok gern bpai
overexposed (*photograph*) sǎirng
mâhk bpai
overheat: it's overheating (*car*) krêu-
ung rórn
overland (*travel*) doy-ee tahng bòk
overlook: overlooking the sea morng
hěn wew ta-lay
**overnight: where can we stay over-
night?** rao ja káhng keun dâi têe

nǎi?; **overnight travel** dern tahng
glahng keun
oversleep: I overslept pǒm (chún)
dteun sǎi bpai
overtake sairng
overweight (*person*) ôo-un
owe: how much do I owe you? pǒm
(chún) bpen nêe koon tâo-rài?
own: my own ... ... kǒrng pǒm
(chún) ayng; **are you on your own?**
(*have you come alone*) koon mah kon
dee-o rěu bplào?; **I'm on my own**
(*I've come alone*) pǒm (chún) mah
kon dee-o
owner jâo-kǒrng
oyster hǒy nahng rom

P

pack: a pack of cigarettes boo-rèe
sorng nèung; **I'll go and pack** pǒm
(chún) bpai jùt gra-bpǎo
package (*at post office etc*) hòr
packed lunch ah-hǎhn glahng wun
glòrng
**packed out: the place was packed
out** kon nâirn
packet sorng; **a packet of cigarettes**
boo-rèe sorng nèung
paddle (*noun*) mái pai
paddy field nah
padlock (*noun*) goon-jair
page (*of book*) nâh; **could you page
Mr ...?** chôo-ay hǎh ber toh-ra-sùp
koon ... hâi dôo-ay
pain kwahm jèp bpòo-ut; **I have a
pain here** jèp dtrong née
painful jèp bpòo-ut
painkillers yah ra-ngúp bpòo-ut
paint (*noun*) sěe; **I'm going to do
some painting** (*artist*) pǒm (chún) ja
kěe-un pâhp sěe

paintbrush (*artist's*) pôo-gun
painting (*picture*) pâhp kěe-un
pair kôo; **a pair of shoes** rorng táo
kôo nèung
pajamas sêu-a gahng gayng norn
Pakistan bpah-gee-sa-tǎhn
Pakistani kon bpah-gee-sa-tǎhn
pal gler
palace prá-râht-cha-wung
pale (*colour*) sěe òrn; (*unwell*) nâh
sêet; **pale blue** sěe fáh òrn; **he looks
pale** káo nâh sêet
palm tree dtôn bpah
palpitations gahn dtên ray-o kǒrng
hǒo-a jai
pancake páirn-káyk
panic: don't panic yàh kwǔn sěe-a ná
panties gahng gayng nai sa-dtree
pants (*trousers*) gahng gayng; (*underpants*) gahng gayng nai
panty girdle gahng gayng rút sa-
pôhk
pantyhose tái

papaya ma-la-gor
paper gra-dàht; (*newspaper*) núng-sěu-pim; **a piece of paper** gra-dàht pàirn nèung
paper bag tǒong gra-dàht
paper handkerchiefs gra-dàht chét nâh
paraffin núm mun gáht
parallel: parallel to ... ka-nǎhn gùp ...
parasol rôm (gun dàirt)
parcel hòr
pardon (me)? (*didn't understand*) a-rai ná?
parents: my parents pôr-mâir kǒrng pǒm (chún)
parents-in-law (*wife's parents*) pôr dtah mâir yai; (*husband's parents*) pôr pǒo-a mâir pǒo-a
park (*noun*) sǒo-un sǎh-tah-ra-ná; **Lumpini Park** sǒo-un lòom-pi-nee
park (*verb*) jòrt; **where can I park?** jòrt dâi têe nǎi?; **there's nowhere to park** mâi mee têe jòrt
parking lights fai jòrt
parking lot têe jòrt rót
parking place: there's a parking place! mee têe jòrt têe nôhn!
part (*noun*) sòo-un
partner (*boyfriend, girlfriend etc*) fairn; (*in business*) pêu-un rôo-um ngahn
party (*group*) glòom kon; (*celebration*) ngahn lée-ung; **let's have a party** jùt ngahn lée-ung dee mái?
pass (*in mountains*) chôrng kǎo; (*verb: overtake*) sairng; **he passed out** káo mòt sa-dtì; **he made a pass at me** káo dtòok dtìk chún
passable (*road*) rót pàhn dâi
passenger pôo doy-ee sǎhn
passport núng-sěu derng tahng
past: in the past mêu-a gòrn; **just past the bank** ler-ee ta-na-kahn bpai èek nít nèung; *see page 112*
pastry (*dough*) bpâirng ka-nǒm; (*small cake*) ka-nǒm
patch: could you put a patch on this? chôo-ay bpà roy kàht hâi nòy dâi mái?

path tahng
patient: be patient jai yen yen
patio ra-bee-ung
pattern bàirp (yàhng); **a dress pattern** bàirp sêu-a
paunch poong
pavement (*sidewalk*) bàht wít-těe
pavilion sǎh-lah
pawnshop rohng rúp jum-num
pay (*verb*) jài; **can I pay, please?** kǒr bin nòy; **it's already paid for** jài láir-o; **I'll pay for this** pǒm (chún) jài ayng
pay phone toh-ra-sùp sǎh-tah-ra-ná
peace and quiet sa-ngòp ngêe-up dee
peanuts tòo-a li-sǒng
pearl kài móok
peas tòo-a
peculiar (*taste, custom*) bplàirk
pedal (*accelerator*) kun rêng; (*bicycle*) kun tèep
pedestrian kon dern táo
pedestrian crossing tahng máh-lai
pedestrian precinct têe hâhm rót kâo
pee: I need to go for a pee pǒm (chún) dtôrng bpai chèe
peeping Tom kon chôrp àirp doo pôo-yǐng gâir pâh
peg (*for washing*) mái nèep
pen bpàhk-gah; **do you have a pen?** mee bpàhk-gah mái?
pencil din-sǒr
penfriend pêu-un tahng jòt-mǎi; **shall we be penfriends?** rao bpen pêu-un tahng jòt-mǎi gun mái?
penicillin yah pen-ni-sin-lin
penknife mêet púp
pen pal pêu-un tahng jòt-mǎi
pension (*from government*) bum-nahn
people kon; **a lot of people** lǎi kon; **the Thai people** kon tai
pepper (*spice*) prík tai; **green pepper** prík yòo-uk; **red pepper** prík yòo-uk dairng
per: ... per night keun la ...; **how much per hour?** chôo-a mohng la tâo-rài?
per cent bper-sen

perfect yôrt yîam
perfume núm hŏrm
perhaps bahng tee
period (*of time*) chôo-a rá-yá; (*menstruation*) bpra-jum deu-un
perm dùt pŏm
permit (*noun*) bai à-nóo-yâht
person kon
perspire ngèu-a òrk
pessimistic morng lôhk nai ngâir rái
petrol núm mun
petrol can gra-bpŏrng núm mun
petrol station púm núm mun
petrol tank (*in car*) tŭng núm mun
pharmacy hâhng kăi yah
phone *see* **telephone**
photogenic tài rôop kêun
photograph (*noun*) rôop-tài; (*verb*) tài rôop; **would you take a photograph of us?** chôo-ay tài rôop rao hâi nòy dâi mái?
photographer châhng tài rôop
phrase: a useful phrase wa-lee têe mee bpra-yòht
phrasebook kôo meu sŏn-ta-nah
pianist núk bpee-a-noh
piano bpee-a-noh
pickpocket ka-moy-ee lóo-ung gra-bpăo
pick up: when can I pick them up? (*clothes from laundry etc*) mah rúp dâi mêu-rài?; **can you come and pick me up?** mah rúp pŏm (chún) dâi mái?
picnic (*noun*) pík-ník
picture rôrp
pie pai
piece chín; **a piece of ...** ... chín nèung
pig mŏo
pigeon nók pi-râhp
piles (*medical*) rôhk rít sĕe doo-ung ta-wahn
pile-up (*crash*) rót chon gun
pill yah mét; **contraceptive pill** yah koom gum-nèrt; **I'm on the pill** chún chái yah koom gum-nèrt
pillarbox dtôo bprai-sa-nee
pillow mŏrn

pillow case bplòrk mŏrn
pin (*noun*) kĕm mòot
pineapple sùp-bpa-rót
pink sĕe chom-poo
pint *see page 115*
pipe (*for smoking*) glôrng yah sòop; (*for water*) bpáirp náhm
pipe cleaner mái tum kwahm sà-aht glôrng yah sòop
pipe tobacco yah glôrng
pity: it's a pity nâh sĕe-a dai
pizza pee-sâh
place (*noun*) sa-tăhn-têe; **is this place taken?** têe nêe wâhng mái?; **would you keep my place for me?** chôo-ay fâo têe née hâi nòy dâi mái?; **at my place** (*home*) têe bâhn pŏm (chún)
place mat têe rorng jahn
plain (*food*) tum-ma-dah; (*not patterned*) mâi mee lôo-ut lai
plane krêu-ung bin
plant dtôn mái
plaster cast fèu-uk
plastic pláir-sa-tìk
plastic bag tŏong pláir-sa-tìk
plate jahn
platform chahn cha-lah; **which platform, please?** chahn cha-lah năi?
play (*verb*) lên; (*noun: in theatre*) la-korn
playboy play-boy
playground sa-năhm dèk lên
pleasant jàirm săi
please: yes please dee see krúp (kâ); **could you please ...?** chôo-ay ... nòy dâi mái?; **can I ... please?** kŏr ... nòy, dâi mái?
plenty: plenty of ... ... mâhk; **that's plenty, thanks** por láir-o kòrp-koon
pleurisy rôhk yêu-a hôom bpòrt ùk-sàyp
pliers keem bpàhk kêep
plug (*electrical, in sink*) bplúk; (*for car*) hŏo-a tee-un
plughole chôrng náhm long
plumber châhng bpra-bpah
plus bòo-uk
p.m.: at 2.00 p.m. bài sŏrng mohng; **at 10.00 p.m.** sèe tôom; *see page 112*

pneumonia bpòrt ùk-sàyp

pocket gra-bpǎo; **in my pocket** nai gra-bpǎo pǒm (chún)

pocketbook (*woman's handbag*) gra-bpǎo těu

pocketknife mêet pók

point: could you point to it? chôo-ay chée hâi nòy dâi mái?; **four point six** sèe jòot hòk; **there's no point** mâi mee bpra-yòht

points (*in car*) torng kǎo

poisonous bpen pít

police dtum-ròo-ut; **call the police!** rêe-uk dtum-ròo-ut mah!

policeman dtum-ròo-ut

police station sa-tǎhn-nee dtum-ròo-ut

polish (*noun*) yah kùt; **will you polish my shoes?** chôo-ay kùt rorng táo hâi nòy dâi mái?

polite soo-pâhp

politician núk gahn meu-ung

politics gahn meu-ung

polluted sěe-a

pomelo sôm oh

pond sà

pony máh glàirp

pool (*for swimming*) sà wâi náhm; (*game*) poon

pool table dtóh bin-lee-ut

poor (*not rich*) jon; (*quality*) mâi ao nǎi; **poor old Somchai!** tôh sǒm-chai ěr-ee!

Pope bpóhp

pop music playng bpóp

poppy dòrk fìn

Popsicle (*tm*) ai-sa-kreem tâirng

pop singer núk rórng

popular bpen têe nee-yom

population bpra-chah-gorn

pork néu-a mǒo

port (*for boats*) tâh reu-a; (*drink*) lâo pòrt

porter (*in hotel*) kon fâo bpra-dtoo; (*at station etc*) pa-núk ngahn rót fai

portrait pâhp kěe-un dtoo-a jing

poser (*phoney person*) kon kêe oh

posh (*restaurant, people*) rǒo-rǎh

possible bpen bpai dâi; **is it possible to ...?** ... bpen bpai dâi mái?; **as ... as possible** yàhng ... têe sòot têe ja ... dâi

post (*noun: mail*) bprai-sa-nee; **could you post this for me?** chôo-ay sòng jòt-mǎi née hâi nòy dâi mái?

postbox dtôo bprai-sa-nee

postcard póht-káht

poster bai bpra-gàht kôht-sa-nah

poste restante 'poste restante'

post office bprai-se-nee

pot (*cooking*) môr; (*tea*) gah núm chah; **pots and pans** (*cooking implements*) môr kâo môr gairng

potato mun fa-rùng

potato chips mun fa-rùng tôrt

pottery (*objects*) krêu-ung bpûn din pǎo; (*workshop*) rohng tum krêu-ung bpûn din pǎo

pound (*money*) bporn; *see page 114*

pour: it's pouring down fǒn dtòk nùk

powder (*for face*) bpâirng

powdered milk nom pǒng

power cut dtùt fai

power point bplúk fai

power station rohng fai fáh

practise, practice: I need to practise pǒm (chún) dtôrng fèuk gòrn

prawn cocktail prórn kórk-tayn

prawns gôong; **barbecued prawns** gôong pǎo

pray sòo-ut mon

prefer chôrp ... mâhk gwàh; **I prefer Thai food** pǒm (chún) chôrp ah-hǎhn tai mâhk gwàh

preferably: preferably not tomorrow kǒr mâi bpen prôong née

pregnant mee tórng

prescription (*for chemist*) bai sùng yah

present (*gift*) kǒrng kwǔn; **here's a present for you** nêe kǒrng kwǔn sǔm-rùp koon; **at present** děe-o née

president (*of company*) bpra-tahn; (*of society, organization*) nah-yók; (*of country*) bpra-tah-nah-tí-bor-dee

press: could you press these? chôo-ay rêet hâi nòy dâi mái?

pretty sǒo-ay; **it's pretty expensive**

pairng mĕu-un gun ná
price rah-kah
prickly heat pòt; **I've got prickly
heat** pŏm (chún) bpen pòt
priest prá
prime minister nah-yók rút-ta-mon-
dtree
prince jâo-fáh chai
princess jâo-fáh yĭng
print (*noun: picture*) rôop ùt
printed matter sìng dtee pim
priority (*in driving*) sìt pàhn bpai
gòrn; **I had priority** pŏm (chún)
mee sìt pàhn bpai gòrn
prison kóok
private sòo-un dtoo-a; **private bathroom** hôrng náhm sòo-un dtoo-a
prize rahng-wun
probably kong-ja
problem bpun-hăh; **I have a problem**
pŏm (chún) mee bpun-hăh; **no
problem!** mâi mee bpun-hăh!
profession ah-chêep
profit gum-rai
program(me) (*noun*) bproh-grairm
progress (*verb*) gâo-nâh; (*noun*)
kwahm ja-rern
prohibit hâhm
promise: **I promise** pŏm (chún) sŭn-
yah; **is that a promise?** sŭn-yah lĕr?
pronounce: **how do you pronounce
this?** kum née òrk sĕe-ung yung-
ngai?
properly: **it's not repaired properly**
mâi dâi sôrm hâi rêe-up róy
prostitute sŏh-pay-nee
protect bpôrng gun

Protestant krít-tee-un
proud poom-jai
province jung-wùt; **Chiangmai
Province** jung-wùt chee-ung-mài
public (*adjective*) săh-tah-ra-ná; (*noun*)
bpra-chah-chon
public convenience sôo-um săh-tah-
ra-ná
public holiday wun yòot râht ha-
gahn
pudding ka-nŏm
pull deung; **he pulled out without
indicating** káo òrk rót doy-ee mâi
dâi hâi sŭn-yahn
pullover sêu-a sa-wét-dtêr
pump (*noun*) sòop
punctual dtrong way-lah
puncture (*noun*) yahng dtàirk
pure (*silk etc*) bor-ri-sòot
purple sĕe môo-ung
purse (*for money*) gra-bpăo sa-dtung;
(*handbag*) gra-bpăo tĕu
push plùk; **don't push in!** yàh sairng
kew!
push-chair rót kĕn
put (*in something*) sài; (*lay down*)
wahng; **where did you put ...?** ... ao
bpai sài/wahng têe năi?; **where can I
put ...?** ... sài/wahng dâi têe năi?;
could you put the lights on? chôo-
ay bpèrt fai nòy dâi mái?; **will you
put the light out?** chôo-ay bpìt fai
dôo-ay; **you've put the price up**
koon kêun rah-kah èek láir-o; **could
you put us up for the night?** kŏr
káhng keun têe nêe nòy dâi mái?
pyjamas sêu-a gahng gayng norn

Q

quality koon-na-pâhp; **poor quality** koon-na-pâhp lay-o; **good quality** koon-na-pâhp dee

quarantine (*place*) dâhn gùk rôhk; (*period*) ra-yá way-lah têe gùk rôhk wái

quart *see page 115*

quarter nèung nai sèe; **quarter of an hour** sìp-hâh nah-tee; *see page 112*

quay tâh reu-a

quayside: on the quayside têe tâh reu-a

queen pra-rah-chi-nee

question kum tăhm; **that's out of the question** bpen bpai mâi dâi

queue (*noun*) kew; **there was a big queue** mee kew yao

quick ray-o; **that was quick** ray-o jing; **which is the quickest way?** bpai tahng năi ray-o têe sòot?

quickly ray-o

quiet (*place, hotel*) ngêe-up; **be quiet!** ngêe-up ngêe-up nòy!

quinine yah kwin-neen

quite: quite a lot mâhk por sŏm-koo-un; **it's quite different** bpen kon la yàhng; **I'm not quite sure** pŏm (chún) mâi kôy nâir jai

R

rabbit gra-dtai

rabies rôhk gloo-a náhm

race (*ethnic*) chéu-a châht; (*sport*) gahn kàirng kŭn

race track sa-năhm máh

racket (*sport*) mái dtee

radiator (*of car, in room*) môr náhm

radio wít-ta-yóo; **on the radio** tahng wít-ta-yóo

rag (*for cleaning*) pâh kêe réw

rail: by rail doy-ee rót fai

railroad, railway tahng rót fai

railroad crossing têe kâhm tahng rót fai

rain (*noun*) fŏn; **in the rain** dtàhk fŏn; **it's raining** fŏn dtòk

rain boots rorng táo bóot

raincoat sêu-a fŏn

rainy season nâh fŏn

rambutan (*fruit*) ngór

rape (*verb*) kòm-kĕun

rare (*object etc*) hăh yâhk; (*steak*) sòok sòok dìp dìp

rash (*on skin*) pèun; **I've got a rash** pŏm (chún) bpen pèun

rat nŏo

rate (*for changing money*) ùt-dtrah; **what's the rate for the pound?** ùt-dtrah lâirk bplèe-un ngern bporn tâo-rài?; **what are your rates?** (*at car hire etc*) koon kít kâh chôo-a mohng la tâo-rài?

rather: it's rather expensive kôrn kâhng ja pairng; **I'd rather ...** pŏm

(chún) yàhk ja ... dee gwàh; **I'd
rather have boiled rice** pŏm (chún)
yàhk ja ao kâo sŏo-ay mâhk gwàh
raw (*meat*) dìp
razor (*dry, electric*) mêet gohn
razor blades bai mêet gohn
reach (*arrive in*) tĕung; **when do we
reach Phuket?** tĕung poo-gèt gèe
mohng?; **within easy reach** bpai
tĕung dâi sa-dòo-uk
read àhn; **I can't read it** pŏm (chún)
àhn mâi òrk; **could you read it out?**
chôo-ay àhn hâi fung nòy dâi mái?
ready (*finished*) sèt; **when will it be
ready?** sèt mêu-a rài?; **I'll go and
get ready** dĕe-o pŏm (chún) ja bpai
dtree-um dtoo-a; **I'm not ready yet**
pŏm (chún) yung mâi sèt
real jing
really jing jing; **I really must go** pŏm
(chún) dtôrng bpai jing jing; **is it
really necessary?** mun jum-bpen
jing jing lĕr?; **really?** jing lĕr?
realtor dtoo-a tairn séu kǎi bâhn
rear: at the rear kâhng lǔng
rear wheels lór lǔng
rearview mirror gra-jòk lǔng
reasonable: reasonable prices rah-
kah yao
receipt bai sèt rúp ngern
receive rúp
recently mêu-a ray-o ray-o née
reception (*in hotel*) pa-nàirk dtôrn
rúp; (*for guests*) ngahn lée-ung dtôrn
rúp
reception desk pa-nàirk dtôrn rúp
receptionist pa-núk ngahn dtôrn rúp
recipe dtum-rah gùp kâo; **can you
give me the recipe for this?** chôo-ay
bòrk wít-tee tum hâi nòy dâi mái?
recognize jum dâi; **I didn't recognize
it** pŏm (chún) jum mâi dâi
**recommend: could you recommend
...?** koon náir-num ... dâi mái?
record (*music*) jahn sĕe-ung
record player krêu-ung lên jahn
sĕe-ung
red sĕe dairng
**reduce: could you reduce the price a

little, please? chôo-ay lót rah-kah
nòy dâi mái?
reduction (*in price*) gahn lót rah-kah
red wine lâo wai dairng
refreshing sòt chêun
refrigerator dtôo yen
refund keun ngern; **do I get a refund?** keun ngern hâi rĕu bplào?
region pâhk
register (*mail, car etc*) long ta-bee-un
registered: by registered mail jòt-mǎi
long ta-bee-un; **I want to send this
letter by registered mail** jòt-mǎi née
pŏm (chún) kŏr sòng long ta-bee-un
registration number ta-bee-un rót
relative: my relatives yâht kŏrng
pŏm (chún)
relaxing: it's very relaxing pòrn klai
ah-rom dee mâhk
reliable (*person, car*) wái jai dâi
religion sǎh-sa-nǎh; **the Buddhist religion** sǎh-sa-nǎh póot
remains (*of old city etc*) sâhk sa-lùk
hùk pung
remember: I don't remember pŏm
(chún) jum mâi dâi; **I remember**
pŏm (chún) jum dâi; **do you remember?** jum dâi mái?
remote (*village etc*) hàhng glai
rent (*noun: for apartment etc*) kâh châo;
(*verb: car etc*) châo; **I'd like to rent a
motorbike/car** pŏm (chún) yàhk ja
châo mor-dter sai/rót
rental car rót châo
repair (*verb*) sôrm; **can you repair it?**
sôrm dâi mái?
repeat pôot èek tee; **could you repeat
that?** pôot èek tee dâi mái?
representative (*noun: of company*) pôo
tairn
request (*verb*) kŏr rórng
rescue (*verb*) chôo-ay chee-wít hâi pón
pai
reservation: I have a reservation
pŏm (chún) dâi jorng wái láir-o
reserve jorng; **I reserved a room in
the name of ...** pŏm (chún) dâi
jorng hôrng nai nahm kŏrng ...; **can
I reserve a table for tonight?** pŏm

(chún) kŏr jorng dtó sǔm-rùp keun née dâi mái?

rest (*repose*) púk pòrn; (*remainder*) têe lěu-a; **I need a rest** pŏm (chún) dtôrng púk pòrn; **the rest of the group** pôo-uk têe lěu-a

restaurant ráhn ah-hǎhn

rest room hôrng náhm

retired: I'm retired pŏm (chún) ga-see-un

return: a return to Bangkok dtŏo-a bpai glùp groong-tâyp; **I'll return it tomorrow** pŏm (chún) ja keun hâi prôong née

returnable: is the deposit returnable? kâh mút-jum keun dâi mái?

reverse charge call toh-ra-sùp gèp ngern bplai tahng

reverse gear gee-a tŏy lŭng

revolting nâh rung-gèe-ut

rheumatism rôhk bpòo-ut nai kôr

rib sêe krohng; **a cracked rib** sêe krohng hùk

ribbon (*for hair*) rib-bîn

rice kâo

rice field nah

rich (*person*) roo-ay; (*food*) mun; **it's too rich** ah-hǎhn mun gern bpai

ride: can you give me a ride into town? chôo-ay pah bpai sòng têe dtoo-a meu-ung dâi mái?; **thanks for the ride** kòrp-koon têe mah sòng

ridiculous: that's ridiculous mâi bpen rêu-ung

right (*correct*) tòok; (*not left*) kwǎh; **you're right** koon tòok láir-o; **you were right** koon tòok láir-o; **that's right** tòok láir-o; **that can't be right** mâi tòok nâir nâir; **right!** (*OK*) ao lá; **is this the right road for ...?** bpai ... tahng ta-nǒn née tòok mái?; **on the right** tahng kwǎh; **turn right** lée-o kwǎh; **not right now** yung mâi ao děe-o née; **right here** (*just here*) dtrong née

right-hand drive poo-ung ma-lai kwǎh

ring (*on finger*) wǎirn; **I'll ring you** pŏm (chún) ja toh bpai těung

ripe (*fruit*) sòok

rip-off: it's a rip-off lòrk dtôm; **rip-off prices** rah-kah lòrk dtôm

risky sèe-ung; **it's too risky** sèe-ung gern bpai

river mâir náhm; **by the river** kâhng kâhng mâir náhm

road ta-nǒn; **is this the road to ...?** nêe ta-nǒn bpai ... châi mái?; **further down the road** ler-ee bpai èek

road accident rót chon gun

road map pǎirn-têe ta-nǒn

roadside: by the roadside kâhng ta-nǒn

roadsign krêu-ung mǎi ja-rah-jorn

roadwork(s) gahn sôrm ta-nǒn

roast (*in an oven*) òp; (*over an open fire*) yâhng; **roast/barbecued chicken** gài yâhng

rob: I've been robbed pŏm (chún) tòok ka-moy-ee

robe (*housecoat*) sêu-a kloom

rock (*stone*) hǐn; **on the rocks** (*with ice*) sài núm kǎirng

rocky (*coast etc*) kòht hǐn

roll (*bread*) ka-nǒm bpung

Roman Catholic kah-tor-lík, krít-dtung

Rome: when in Rome ... kâo meu-ung dtah lèw dtôrng lèw dtah dtahm

roof lŭng-kah; **on the roof** bon lŭng-kah

roof rack gròrp dtìt lŭng-kah rót

room hôrng; **do you have a room?** mee hôrng wâhng mái?; **a room for three nights** mee hôrng hâi yòo sǎhm wun mái?; **single room** (*one double bed*) hôrng dèe-o; **single room with air-conditioning** hôrng dèe-o bprùp ah-gàht; **double room** (*two single beds*) hôrng kôo; **double room with air-conditioning** hôrng kôo bprùp ah-gàht; **in my room** nai hôrng pŏm (chún); **there's no room** mâi mee têe wâhng

room service bor-ri-gahn rúp chái nai hôrng púk

rope chêu-uk
rose dòrk gOO-làhp
rotary wong wee-un
rough (*sea, crossing*) klêun jùt; **the engine sounds a bit rough** krêu-ung dern mâi rêe-up
roughly (*approximately*) bpra-mahn
roulette roo-lét
round (*adjective*) glom; **it's my round** bpen tee kŏrng pŏm
roundabout (*for traffic*) wong wee-un
round-trip: a round-trip ticket to ... dtŏo-a bpai glùp ...
route tahng; **what's the best route?** bpai tahng nǎi dee têe sòot?
rowboat, rowing boat reu-a pai
royal palace pra-râht-cha-wung
rubber (*material*) yahng; (*eraser*) yahng lóp
rubber band yahng rút

rubbish (*waste*) ka-yà; (*poor quality goods*) kŏrng kOOn-na-pâhp mâi dee; **that's rubbish!** (*nonsense*) mâi bpen rêu-ung!
rucksack bpây lŭng
rude (*impolite*) mâi mee mah-ra-yâht; **he was very rude** káo mâi mee mah-ra-yâht ler-ee
rug prom
ruins sâhk sa-lùk hùk pung
rum lâo rum
rum and coke rum airn kóhk
run (*person*) wîng; **I go running** (*i.e. habitually*) pŏm (chún) bpen núk wîng; **quick, run!** ray-o ray-o kâo wîng!; **how often do the buses run?** rót may wîng tèe mái?; **he's been run over** káo tòok rót chon; **I've run out of gas/petrol** núm mun mòt
Russia bpra-tâyt rút-see-a

S

saccharine sáirk-ka-rin
sad sâo
saddle (*for bike*) ahn rót jùk-gra-yahn; (*for horse*) ahn máh
safe (*not in danger*) bplòrt-pai; (*not dangerous*) mâi un-dta-rai; **will it be safe here?** têe nêe bplòrt-pai mái?; **is it safe to drink?** náhm née bplòrt-pai sŭm-rùp dèum rěu bplào?; **is it a safe beach for swimming?** hàht née bplòrt-pai sŭm-rùp wâi náhm rěu bplào?; **could you put this in your safe?** chôo-ay sài dtôo sáyf hâi nòy, dâi mái?
safety pin kêm glùt
sail (*noun*) bai reu-a; **can we go sailing?** bpai lên reu-a bai gun dâi mái?
sailor (*merchant navy*) ga-lah-sěe; (*armed forces*) ta-hǎhn reu-a
salad sa-lùt

salad cream kreem sa-lùt
salad dressing náhm sa-lùt
salary ngern deu-un
sale: is it for sale? un née kǎi rěu bplào?; **it's not for sale** mâi kǎi
sales clerk pa-núk ngahn kǎi
salmon bplah sairn-morn
salt gleu-a
salty kem; **it's too salty** kem gern bpai
salung (*unit of currency = 25 satang, 1 baht = 4 salung*) sa-lěung
same měu-un gun; **one the same as this** ao měu-un yung ngée; **the same again, please** kŏr yàhng derm; **same to you** kOOn gôr měu-un gun ná; **it's all the same to me** a-rai gôr dâi; **thanks all the same** kòrp-kOOn
sampan reu-a sǔm-bpûn
sand sai

sandal(s) rorng táo dtàir
sandwich sairn-wít; **a chicken sandwich** sairn-wít gài
sandy bpen sai; **a sandy beach** hàht sai
sanitary napkin/towel pâh a-nah-mai
sarcastic bpra-chót
sardines bplah sah-deen
satang (*unit of currency, 100 satang = 1 baht*) sa-dtung
satisfactory bpen têe nâh por jai; **this is not satisfactory** mâi bpen têe nâh por jai
satisfied por jai
Saturday wun săo
sauce núm jîm
saucepan môr
saucer jahn rorng tôo-ay
sauna sor-nâh
sausage sâi gròrk
save (*life*) chôo-ay chee-wít; (*money*) gèp ngern wái
savo(u)ry ah-hăhn kao
say: how do you say ... in Thai? ... pah-săh tai pôot wâh yung-ngai?; **pardon, what did you say?** a-rai ná? kOOn pôot wâh yung-ngai?; **what did he say?** káo pôot wâh yung-ngai?; **I said ...** pŏm (chún) bòrk wâh ...; **he said ...** káo bòrk wâh ...; **I wouldn't say no** (*yes please*) pŏm (chún) mâi bpà-dti-sàyt ròrk
scald: he's scalded himself káo tòok núm rórn lôo-uk
scared gloo-a; **I'm scared of ghosts** pŏm (chún) gloo-a pĕe
scarf (*for neck*) pâh pun kor; (*for head*) pâh pôhk sĕe-sà
scarlet sĕe lêu-ut mŏo
scenery (*views*) poo-mi-bpra-tâyt
scent (*perfume*) núm hŏrm
schedule rai-gahn
scheduled flight têe-o bin
school rohng ree-un; (*university*) ma-hăh-wít-ta-yah-lai; **I'm still at school** pŏm (chún) yung bpen núk ree-un yòo
science wít-ta-yah-sàht
scissors: a pair of scissors gun-grai, dta-grai
scooter (*motor scooter*) rót sa-góot-dter
scorching: it's really scorching (*weather*) dàirt rórn bprêe-ung
score dtâirm; **what's the score?** dâi gèe dtâirm láir-o?
scotch (*whisky*) lâo wít-sa-gêe
Scotch tape (*tm*) sa-górt tâyp
Scotland bpra-tâyt sa-górt-lairn
Scottish kon sa-górt
scratch (*verb*) (*because of itch*) gao; (*oneself on a sharp object*) kòo-un; **it's only a scratch** bpen roy kòo-un tâo-nún
scream (*verb*) wèet rórng
screw (*noun*) dta-bpoo koo-ung
screwdriver kăi koo-ung
scrubbing brush (*for hands*) bprairng tŏo lép; (*for floors*) bprairng tŏo péun
scruffy (*appearance, person, hotel*) mor-sor
sea ta-lay; **by the sea** chai ta-lay
sea air ah-gàht chai ta-lay
seafood ah-hăhn ta-lay
seafood restaurant pút-ta-kahn ah-hăhn ta-lay
seafront chai ta-lay; **on the seafront** chai ta-lay
seagull nók nahng noo-un
search (*verb*) hăh; **I searched everywhere** pŏm (chún) bpai hăh tóok hòn tóok hàirng
search party ka-ná pôo kón hăh
seashell bplèu-uk hŏy
seasick: I feel seasick pŏm (chún) róo-sèuk mao klêun; **I get seasick** pŏm (chún) mao klêun ngâi
seaside: by the seaside chai ta-lay; **let's go to the seaside** bpai têe-o chai ta-lay mái?
season (*colloquial word*) nâh; (*formal word*) reu-doo; **cool season** nâh năo; **hot season** nâh rórn; **rainy season** nâh fŏn; **in the high season** reu-doo núk tôrng têe-o mâhk; **in the low season** reu-doo núk tôrng têe-o nóy
seasoning krêu-ung choo rót
seat têe nûng; **is this anyone's seat?**

têe nûng née wâhng rěu bplào?;
seat belt têe rút kěm kùt; **do you
have to wear a seat belt?** dtôrng rút
kěm kùt rěu bplào?
sea urchin bpling ta-lay
seaweed sǎh-rài-ta-lay
secluded dòht dèe-o
second (*adjective*) têe sǒrng; (*of time*)
wí-nah-tee; **just a second!** děe-o
gòrn!; **can I have a second helping?**
kǒr dterm nòy dâi mái?
second class (*travel*) chún sǒrng
secret (*noun*) kwahm lúp
secretary (*in an office*) lay-kǎh-nóo-
gahn
security check dtròo-ut kwahm
bplòrt-pai
sedative yah ra-ngúp bpra-sàht
see hěn; **I didn't see it** pǒm (chún)
mâi hěn; **have you seen my husband?** kOOn hěn sǎh-mee chún mái?;
I saw him this morning hěn mêu-a
cháo née; **can I see the manager?**
kǒr póp pôo-jùt-gahn nòy, dâi mái?;
see you tonight! keun née póp gun
ná; **can I see?** kǒr doo nòy, dâi
mái?; **oh, I see** (*I understand*) ôh, kâo
jai láir-o; **will you see to it?** (*arrange
it*) chôo-ay jùt gahn hâi nòy ná
seldom mâi bòy
selfish hěn gàir dtoo-a
self-service bor-ri-gahn chôo-ay
dtoo-a ayng
sell kǎi; **do you sell ...?** mee ... kǎi
mái?; **will you sell it to me?** kOOn
ja kǎi hâi pǒm (chún) mái?
sellotape (*tm*) sa-górt tâyp
send sòng; **I want to send this to
England** pǒm (chún) yàhk ja sòng
nêe bpai ung-grìt; **I'll have to send
this food back** ja dtôrng sòng ah-
hǎhn née keun
senior citizen kon cha-rah
sensational (*holiday, experience etc*) wí-
sàyt
sense: I have no sense of direction
pǒm (chún) mâi róo rêu-ung tít-
tahng; **it doesn't make sense** mâi
bpen rêu-ung

sensible (*person, idea*) mee hàyt-pǒn
sensitive (*person*) kon mee ah-rom
òrn-wǎi; (*skin*) pěw bahng
sentimental la-èe-ut òrn
separate (*verb*) yâirk gun; **can we
have separate bills?** chôo-ay kít
ngern yâirk gun
separated: I'm separated (*man*) pǒm
yâirk gun gùp pun-ra-yah; (*woman*)
chún yâirk gun gùp sǎh-mee
separately (*pay, travel*) yâirk gun
September gun-yah-yon
septic mee chéu-a
serious (*person*) ao jing ao jung;
(*situation*) dtreung krêe-ut; (*problem,
illness*) nùk; **I'm serious** pǒm (chún)
pôot jing jing ná; **you can't be serious!** ja bpen bpai dâi yung-ngai?; **is
it serious, doctor?** bpen nùk jing
jing rěu kOOn mǒr?
seriously: seriously ill bpòo-ay nùk
servant kon chái
service bor-ri-gahn; **the service was
excellent** bor-ri-gahn yôrt yêe-um;
could we have some service, please!
kǒr bor-ri-gahn nòy; **church service**
sòo-ut mon nai bòht; **the car needs
a service** rót dtôrng dtròo-ut sa-
pâhp
service charge (*in restaurant*) kâh
bor-ri-gahn
service station bpúm núm mun
serviette pâh chét meu
set (*noun: of books, cutlery etc*) chóot;
it's time we were setting off těung
way-lah dtôrng bpai láir-o
set menu ah-hǎhn chóot
settle up: can we settle up now?
(*pay*) kǒr jài děe-o née dâi mái?
several lǎi
sew yép; **could you sew this back
on?** chôo-ay yép hâi nòy dâi mái?
sex (*sexual intercourse*) gahn rôo-um
bpra-way-nee
sexy 'sexy'
shade: in the shade nai rôm
shadow ngao
shake: let's shake hands jùp meu
gun

shallow (*water*) dtêun

shame: what a shame! nâh sĕe-a dai!

shampoo (*noun*) yah sà pŏm; **can I have a shampoo and set?** kŏr sà sét

share (*verb*: *room, table etc*) chái ... rôo-um gun; **let's share the cost** chôo-ay gun jài

shark bplah cha-lăhm

sharp (*knife*) kom; (*taste*) bprêe-o; (*pain*) sĕe-o; **nine o'clock sharp** gâo mohng dtrong

shattered: I'm shattered (*very tired*) pŏm (chún) nèu-ay mâhk

shave gohn; **I need a shave** pŏm dtôrng gohn nòo-ut; **can you give me a shave?** gohn nòo-ut hâi nòy, dâi mái?

shaver krêu-ung gohn nòo-ut

shaving brush bprairng tah kreem gohn nòo-ut

shaving foam kreem gohn nòo-ut

shaving point bplúk krêu-ung gohn nòo-ut

shaving soap sa-bòo gohn nòo-ut

shawl pâh kloom lài

she káo; **is she here?** káo yòo têe nêe mái; **is she a friend of yours?** káo bpen pêu-un koon rĕu bplào?; **she's not English** káo mâi châi kon ung-grìt; *see page 101*

sheet (*for bed*) pâh bpòo têe norn

shelf hîng

shell hŏy

shellfish hŏy

shingles rôhk ngoo sa-wùt

ship reu-a; **by ship** tahng reu-a

shirt sêu-a chért

shit! âi hàh!

shock (*surprise*) dtòk jai; **I got an electric shock from the ...** pŏm (chún) tòok fai chòrk têe ...

shock-absorber chórk

shocking (*behaviour, prices, custom etc*) lĕu-a gern jing jing

shoe rorng táo; **my shoes** rorng táo kŏrng pŏm (chún); **a pair of shoes** rorng táo kôo nèung

shoelaces chêu-uk pòok rorng táo

shoe polish yah kùt rorng táo

shoe repairer kon sôrm rorng táo

shop ráhn

shopping: I'm going shopping pŏm (chún) bpai séu kŏrng

shop window nâh gra-jòk ráhn

shore (*of sea, lake*) fùng

short (*in length*) sûn; **a short person** kon dtêe-a; **a short time** way-lah mâi nahn; **a short journey** gahn dern tahng ra-yá sûn; **it's only a short distance** yòo mâi glai

short-change: you've short-changed me koon torn ngern hâi mâi króp

short circuit fai chórt

shortcut tahng lút

shorts gahng gayng kăh sûn; (*underwear*) gahng gayng nai

should koo-un ja; **what should I do?** pŏm (chún) koo-un ja tum yung-ngai?; **he shouldn't be long** káo mâi koo-un ja cháh; **you should have told me** koon koo-un ja bòrk pŏm (chún) gòrn

shoulder lài

shoulder blade bpàh

shout (*verb*) dta-gohn

show: could you show me? kŏr doo nòy; **does it show?** morng hĕn mái?; **we'd like to go to a show** rao yàhk ja bpai doo gahn sa-dairng

shower (*in bathroom*) fùk boo-a; **with shower** mee fùk boo-a

showercap mòo-uk àhp náhm

show-off: don't be a show-off yàh kee òo-ut hâi mâhk ná

shrimps gôong

shrine sa-tăhn sùk-gah-rá

shrink: it's shrunk hòt láir-o

shut (*verb*) bpìt; **when do you shut?** koon bpìt gèe mohng?; **when do they shut?** káo bpìt gèe mohng?; **it was shut** bpìt láir-o; **I've shut myself out** leum ao goon-jair òrk mah; **shut up!** yòot pôot ná!

shutter (*on camera*) 'shutter'; (*on window*) a-lùk nâh-dtàhng

shy ai

sick (*ill*) mâi sa-bai; **I think I'm going to be sick** (*vomit*) róo-sèuk wâh klêun sâi; **I'm sick of ...** pǒm (chún) bèu-a ...

side kâhng; (*in game*) teem; **at the side of the road** kâhng ta-nǒn; **the other side of town** èek fâhk nèung kǒrng meu-ung

side lights fai kâhng

side salad sa-lùt

side street soy

sidewalk bàht wí-těe

sidewalk café ráhn gǒo-ay dtěe-o

sight: the sights of ... sa-tǎhn-têe nâh têe-o nai ...

sightseeing: sightseeing tour rai-gahn num têe-o; **we're going sightseeing** rao ja bpai têe-o

sign (*roadsign etc*) bpâi sǔn-yahn ja-rah-jorn; (*written character*) bpâi; **where do I sign?** pǒm (chún) sen chêu têe nǎi?

signal: he didn't give a signal (*driver, cyclist*) káo mâi dâi hâi sǔn-yahn

signature lai sen

signpost dtùt bpâi ja-rah-jorn

silence kwahm ngêe-up

silencer krêu-ung gèp sěe-ung

silent ngêe-up

silk mǎi; **Thai silk** mǎi tai

silly (*person, thing to do etc*) ngôh; **that's silly!** mâi bpen rêu-ung!

silver ngern

silver foil gra-dàht dta-gòo-a

silversmith châhng ngern

similar měu-un

simple (*easy*) ngâi

since: since yesterday dtûng-dtàir mêu-a wahn née; **since we got here** dtûng-dtàir rao mah těung

sincere jing jai

sing rórng playng

singer núk rórng

single: a single room hôrng dèe-o; **a single to ...** dtǒo-a bpai ...; **I'm single** pǒm (chún) bpen sòht

sink (*basin*) àhng; **it sank** jom náhm

sister: older sister pêe sǎo; **younger sister** nórng sǎo; **my older/younger sister** pêe/nórng sǎo kǒrng pǒm (chún)

sister-in-law: my older sister-in-law pêe sa-pái kǒrng pǒm (chún); **my younger sister-in-law** nórng sa-pái kǒrng pǒm (chún)

sit nûng; **may I sit here?** kǒr nûng têe nêe, dâi mái?; **is anyone sitting here?** mee kon nûng têe nêe rěu bplào?; **please sit down** chern nûng see

situation sa-tǎhn-na-gahn

size ka-nàht; **do you have any other sizes?** mee ka-nàht èun mái?

sketch (*noun*) pâhp wâht

skid: I skidded rót cha-làirp

skin (*of person*) pěw, pěw-nǔng; (*of animal*) nǔng; (*of fruit*) bplèu-uk

skin-diving gahn dum náhm léuk; **I'm going skin-diving** pǒm (chún) bpai dum náhm léuk

skinny pǒrm

skirt gra-bprohng

skull gra-lòhk sěe-sà

sky fáh

sleep norn lùp; **I can't sleep** pǒm (chún) norn mâi lùp; **did you sleep well?** lùp dee mái?; **I need a good sleep** pǒm (chún) dtôrng-gahn bpai norn hâi mâhk mâhk

sleeper (*train*) dtôo norn

sleeping bag tǒong norn

sleeping car (*rail*) rót norn

sleeping pill yah norn lùp

sleepy (*person*) ngôo-ung norn; (*town*) ngêe-up; **I'm feeling very sleepy** pǒm (chún) róo-sèuk ngôo-ung norn mâhk

sleeve kǎirn sêu-a

slice (*noun*) pàirn

slide (*photograph*) 'slide'

slim (*adjective*) pree-o; **I'm slimming** pǒm (chún) gum-lung lót núm-nùk

slip (*under dress*) gra-bprohng chún nai; **I slipped** (*on pavement etc*) pǒm (chún) lêun

slippery lêun; **it's slippery** lêun

slow cháh; **slow down!** (*driving*) kùp cháh cháh nòy; (*speaking*) pôot cháh cháh nòy!

slowly cháh cháh; **could you say it**

slowly? pôot cháh cháh nòy dâi
mái?; **very slowly** cháh mâhk
small lék
small change sàyt sa-dtung
smallpox kâi tor-ra-pít
smart (*clothes*) găy găi; (*clever*) cha-làht
smashing (*holiday, time, food etc*) yôrt
smell (*verb*) (*with the nose*) dâi glìn; (*have bad smell*) měn; **I think I can smell something** róo-sèuk dâi glìn a-rai bahng yàhng; **what a lovely smell!** hŏrm jung ler-ee!; **it smells (bad)** měn; **there's a funny smell** mee glìn bpra-làht
smile (*verb*) yím
smoke (*noun*) kwun; **do you smoke?** kOOn sòop bOO-rèe mái?; **do you mind if I smoke?** kŏr sòop bOO-rèe dâi mái?; **I don't smoke** pŏm (chún) mâi sòop bOO-rèe
smooth (*surface*) rêe-up
snack: I'd just like a snack kŏr ah-hǎhn wâhng nòy
snails hŏi tâhk
snake ngoo
sneakers rorng-táo pâh bai
snob kon hŏo-a sŏong
snow (*noun*) hi-má
so: it's so hot rórn jung ler-ee; **it was so beautiful!** sŏo-ay jung ler-ee; **not so fast** yàh ray-o núk; **thank you so much** kòrp-kOOn mâhk mâhk; **it wasn't — it was so!** mâi châi — châi see!; **so am I** pŏm (chún) gôr měu-un gun; **so do I** pŏm (chún) gôr měu-un gun; **how was it? — so-so** bpen yung-ngai? — gôr yàhng nún làir
soaked: I'm soaked pŏm (chún) bpèe-uk chôhk
soaking solution (*for contact lenses*) núm yah láhng korn-táirk layn
soap sa-bòo
soap-powder pŏng súk fôrk
sober (*not drunk*) mâi mao
sober up sàhng mao
soccer fóot-born
sock tŏong-táo
socket (*electrical*) bplúk fai

soda (water) núm soh-dâh
sofa gâo-êe rúp kàirk
soft (*material etc*) nîm
soft drink náhm kòo-ut
soft lenses 'soft lenses'
soldier ta-hǎhn
sole (*of shoe*) péun rórng táo; **could you put new soles on these?** sài péun rórng táo mài hâi nòy, dâi mái?
solid kǎirng
some: some people bahng kon; **some things** bahng yàhng; **may I have some water?** kŏr náhm nòy, dâi mái?; **do you have some matches?** mee mái-kèet mái?; **that's some drink!** rairng jung ler-ee!; **some of them** (*people*) bahng kon; (*things*) bahng yàhng; **can I have some?** kŏr nòy, dâi mái?
somebody, someone krai
something a-rai; **something to drink** kŏr a-rai dèum nòy
sometime: sometime this afternoon dtorn bài wun née
sometimes bahng tee
somewhere têe nǎi
son lôok chai; **my son** lôok chai kŏrng pŏm (chún)
song playng
Songkran sŏng-grahn
son-in-law: my son-in-law lôok kěr-ee kŏrng pŏm (chún)
soon děe-o; **I'll be back soon** děe-o glùp ná; **as soon as you can** yàhng ray-o têe sòot têe ja ray-o dâi
sore: it's sore jèp
sore throat: I have a sore throat pŏm (chún) jèp kor
sorry: (I'm) sorry kŏr-tôht; **sorry?** (*didn't understand*) a-rai ná krúp (ká)?
sort: what sort of ...? ... bàirp nǎi?; **a different sort of ...** ... bàirp èun; **will you sort it out?** chôo-ay doo hâi nòy, dâi mái?
sound (*noun*) sěe-ung
soup sóop; **noodle soup** gŏo-ay dtěe-o náhm
sour (*taste*) bprêe-o

south dtâi; **to the south** tahng tít dtâi

South Africa áhf-ri-gah dtâi

South African (*adjective*) áhf-ri-gah dtâi

southeast dta-wun òrk chěe-ung dtâi; **to the southeast** tahng tít dta-wun òrk chěe-ung dtâi

South East Asia ay-see-a ah-ka-nay

southern region (*of Thailand*) pâhk dtâi

South Vietnam wêe-ut nahm dtâi

southwest dta-wun dtòk chěe-ung dtâi; **to the southwest** tahng tít dta-wun dtòk chěe-ung dtâi

souvenir kŏrng têe ra-léuk

soy sauce núm see éw

spade jòrp

spanner goon-jair bpàhk dtai

spare part a-lài

spare ribs sêe krohng mŏo

spare tyre/tire yahng a-lài

spark(ing) plug hŏo-a tee-un

speak pôot; **do you speak English?** koon pôot pah-săh ung-grìt bpen mái?; **I don't speak ...** pŏm (chún) pôot ... mâi bpen; **can I speak to ...?** kŏr pôot gùp ... nòy, dâi mái?; **speaking** (*on telephone*) ... gum-lung pôot

special pi-sàyt; **nothing special** mâi mee a-rai pi-sàyt

specialist (*expert*) pôo chêe-o chahn

special(i)ty (*food*) ah-hăhn pi-sàyt; **the special(i)ty of the house** ah-hăhn pi-sàyt bpra-jum ráhn

spectacles wâirn dtah

speed (*noun*) kwahm ray-o; **he was speeding** káo kùp ray-o gern bpai

speedboat reu-a ray-o

speed limit ùt-dtrah kwahm ray-o

speedometer krêu-ung wút kwahm ray-o

spell: how do you spell it? sa-gòt yung-ngai?

spend chái ngern; **I've spent all my money** pŏm (chún) chái ngern mòt láir-o

spice krêu-ung tâyt

spicy: it's very spicy pèt mâhk

spider mairng moom

splendid (*very good*) yôrt yêe-um

splint (*for broken limb*) fèu-uk

splinter (*in finger*) sa-gèt mái

splitting: I've got a splitting headache pŏm (chún) bpòo-ut hŏo-a mâhk

spoke (*in wheel*) sêe lór

sponge forng náhm

spoon chórn

sport gee-lah

spot (*on face etc*) sěw; **will they do it on the spot?** ja tum hâi děe-o nún mái?

sprain: I've sprained my ... pŏm (chún) tum ... klét

spray (*for hair*) sa-bpay chèet pŏm

spring (*season*) reu-doo bai mái plì; (*of car, seat*) lahn sa-bpring

square: Siam Square sa-yahm sa-kwair; **ten square metres** sìp dta-rahng máyt

squeeze bèep

squid bplah-mèuk

stain (*noun: on clothes*) bpêu-un

stairs bun-dai

stale (*bread, taste*) mâi sòt

stall: the engine keeps stalling krêu-ung dùp bòy

stamp (*noun*) sa-dtairm; **a stamp for England, please** kŏr sa-dtairm sòng bpai ung-grìt

stand (*be standing*) yeun; **I can't stand ...** (*can't tolerate*) pŏm (chún) ton ... mâi dâi

standard (*adjective*) mah-dtra-tăhn

standby 'standby'

star dao; **movie star** dah-rah nǔng

start (*noun*) rêrm; **when does the film start?** nǔng rêrm chǎi mêu-a rài?; **the car won't start** rót sa-dtàht mâi dtìt

starter (*of car*) bpòom sa-dtàht; (*food*) ah-hăhn glâirm

starving: I'm starving pŏm (chún) hěw jung ler-ee

state (*in country*) rút; **the States** (*USA*) sa-hà rút

station (*railway*) sa-tǎhn-nee rót fai;

(*bus*) sa-tăhn-nee rót may; (*police*) sa-tăhn-nee dtum-ròo-ut
statue a-nóo-săh-wa-ree
stay: we enjoyed our stay here rao púk têe nêe sa-nòok mâhk; **where are you staying?** koon púk yòo têe năi?; **I'm staying at ...** pŏm (chún) púk yòo têe ...; **I'd like to stay another week** pŏm (chún) yàhk ja yòo dtòr èek ah-tít nèung; **I'm staying in tonight** keun née pŏm (chún) mâi òrk bpai năi
steak néu-a sa-dték
steal ka-moy-ee; **my bag has been stolen** gra-bpăo tòok ka-moy-ee
steam ai náhm
steep (*hill*) chun
steering: the steering is slack poo-ung ma-lai lŏo-um
steering wheel poo-ung ma-lai
step (*in front of house etc*) kûn bun-dai
stereo sa-tay-ri-oh
sterling (*currency*) ngern bporn
stew sa-dtoo
steward (*on plane*) pa-núk ngahn krêu-ung bin
stewardess 'air hostess'
sticking plaster plah-sa-dter
sticky: it's sticky něe-o
sticky rice kâo něe-o
sticky tape tâyp něe-o
still: I'm still waiting pŏm (chún) yung ror yòo; **will you still be open?** koon ja yung bpèrt yòo rěu bplào?; **it's still not right** yung mâi tòok; **that's still better** yîng dee gwàh; **keep still!** yòo nîng nîng!
sting (*verb*) dtòy; **a bee sting** roy pêung dtòy; **I've been stung** pŏm (chún) tòok ma-lairng dtòy
stink (*verb*) mĕn; **it stinks** mĕn
stockings tŏong nôrng
stolen tòok ka-moy-ee; **my wallet's been stolen** gra-bpăo sa-dtahng pŏm (chún) tòok ka-moy-ee
stomach tórng; **do you have something for an upset stomach?** mee yah gâir tórng sěe-a mái?
stomach-ache bpòo-ut tórng
stone (*rock*) hĭn; *see page 114*
stop (*bus stop*) bpâi rót-may; **which stop do I get on at for ...?** bpai ... kêun rót-may têe năi?; **which stop do I get off at for ...?** bpai ... long rót-may têe năi?; **please, stop here** (*to taxi driver etc*) jòrt dtrong née; **do you stop near ...?** koon yòot glâi glâi ... mái?; **stop doing that!** yòot ná!
stopover wáir
store (*shop*) ráhn
stor(e)y (*of building*) chún
storm pah-yóo
story (*tale*) ní-tahn
stove dtao
straight (*road etc*) dtrong dtrong; **it's straight ahead** yòo dtrong nâh; **straight away** tun-tee; **a straight whisky** wít-sa-gêe pee-o
straighten: can you straighten things out? (*sort things out*) chôo-ay gâir kăi hâi nòy, dâi mái?
strange (*odd*) bplàirk; (*unknown*) bplàirk bpra-làht
stranger kon bplàirk nâh; **I'm a stranger here** pŏm (chún) mâi châi kon têe nêe
strap (*on watch, on dress, on suitcase*) săi
strawberry sa-dtor-ber-rêe
steam lum-tahn
street ta-nŏn; **on the street** bon ta-nŏn
street café ráhn gŏo-ay dtěe-o
streetmap păirn-têe ta-nŏn
strep throat jèp kor
strike: they're on strike káo nút yòot ngahn
string chêu-uk; **have you got some string?** mee chêu-uk mái?
striped bpen lai
striptease ra-bum bpóh
stroke: he's had a stroke káo bpen lom bpai
stroll: let's go for a stroll bpai dern lên mái?
stroller (*for babies*) rót kĕn dèk
strong (*person*) kăirng rairng; (*taste*) jùt; (*drink*) gàir; (*curry*) pèt

stroppy (*official, waiter*) mâi soo-pâhp
stuck dtìt; **the key's stuck** goon-jair dtìt káhng yòo
student núk sèuk-săh
stupid ngôh; **that's stupid** ngôh
sty(e) (*in eye*) gôong-ying
subtitles kum bun-yai
suburb bor-ri-wayn chahn meu-ung
successful: were you successful? koon dâi rúp kwahm sŭm-rèt rĕu bplào?
suddenly tun-tee
sue: I intend to sue pŏm (chún) ja fórng
suede nŭng glùp
sugar núm dtahn; **do you take sugar?** sài núm dtahn mái?; **no sugar, thank you** mâi sài núm dtahn, krúp (kâ)
suggest: what do you suggest? koon ja náir-num a-rai?
suit (*noun*) chóot; **it doesn't suit me** mâi mòr gùp pŏm (chún); **it suits you** mòr gùp koon dâi dee; **that suits me fine** mòr dee láir-o
suitable (*convenient*) sa-dòo-uk; (*appropriate*) mòr sŏm
suitcase gra-bpăo dern tahng
sulk: he's sulking káo ngorn
sultry (*weather, climate*) nĕe-o
summer nâh rórn; **in the summer** dtorn nâh rórn
sun prá-ah-tít; **in the sun** dtàhk dàirt; **out of the sun** nai rôm; **I've had too much sun** pŏm (chún) tòok dàirt mâhk bpai
sunbathe àhp dàirt
sunblock (*cream*) yah tah gun dàirt
sunburn mâi dàirt
sunburnt tòok dàirt mâi
Sunday wun ah-tít
sunglasses wâirn gun dàirt
sun lounger (*chair for lying on*) máh nûng àhp dàirt
sunny: if it's sunny tâh dàirt òrk; **a sunny day** wun dàirt òrk; **it's always sunny here** têe nêe dàirt òrk sa-mĕr
sunrise ah-tít kêun

sun roof (*in car*) lŭng-kah gra-jòk
sunset ah-tít dtòk
sunshade ngao dàirt
sunshine dàirt òrk
sunstroke rôhk páir dàirt
suntan pĕw klúm dàirt
suntan lotion kreem tah àhp dàirt
suntanned mee pĕw klúm dàirt
suntan oil núm mun tah àhp dàirt
super (*time, holiday, person*) yôrt yêe-um; **super!** yôrt yêe-um!
superb (*buildings, sunsets, view*) yôrt yêe-um
supermarket soo-bper mah-get
supper ah-hăhn yen
supplement (*extra charge*) kâh bor-ri-gahn pi-sàyt
suppose: I suppose so pŏm (chún) sŏng-săi wâh yung ngún
suppository yah nèp
sure: I'm sure pŏm (chún) nâir-jai; **are you sure?** koon nâir-jai rĕu?; **he's sure** káo nâir-jai; **sure!** nâir-norn!
surname nahm sa-goon
suprised bpra-làht jai; **I was very suprised** pŏm (chún) bpra-làht jai mâhk
suprising: that's not suprising mâi châi rêu-ung nâh bpra-làht
swallow (*verb*) gleun
swamp nŏrng
swearword kum ngèu-a-bòt
sweat (*noun*) ngèu-a; (*verb*) ngèu-a òrk; **covered in sweat** ngèu-a tôo-um
seater sêu-a sa-wet-dter
sweatshirt sêu-a sa-wet-dter
sweet (*taste*) wăhn; (*noun: dessert*) kŏrng wăhn
sweet and sour bprêe-o wăhn
sweet and sour fish bplah bprêe-o wăhn
sweet and sour pork mŏo bprêe-o wăhn
sweets tórp-fêe
swelling boo-um
sweltering: it's sweltering rórn bpen bâh

swerve: I had to swerve (*when driving*) pŏm (chún) dtôrng hùk poo-ung mah-lai

swim (*verb*) wâi náhm; **I'm going for a swim** pŏm (chún) bpai wâi náhm; **do you want to go for a swim?** bpai wâi náhm mái?; **I can't swim** pŏm (chún) wâi náhm mâi bpen

swimming gahn wâi nahm; **I like swimming** pŏm (chún) chôrp wâi náhm

swimming costume chóot àhp náhm

swimming pool sà wâi náhm

swimming trunks gahng gayng wâi náhm

switch (*noun*) sa-wít fai; **could you switch it on?** chôo-ay bpèrt hâi nòy, dâi mái?; **could you switch it off?** chôo-ay bpìt hâi nòy, dâi mái?

swollen boo-um

swollen glands dtòrm boo-um

sympathy kwahm hĕn jai; **I'd like to express my sympathy** kŏr sa-dairng kwahm hĕn jai

synagogue bòht yew

synthetic yai sŭng-krór

T

table dtó; **a table for two** dtó sŭm-rùp sŏrng kon; **can we have our usual table?** kŏr dtó derm

tablecloth pâh bpoo dtó

table tennis bping bporng

tactful (*person*) kon róo-jùk gah-lá tâyt-sà

tailback (*of traffic*) rót dtùt

tailor châhng dtùt sêu-a pâh

take (*something to a place*) ao ... bpai; (*someone to a place*) pah ... bpai; **will you take this to room 12?** chôo-ay ao nêe bpai hôrng sìp-sŏrng nòy, dâi mái?; **will you take me to the airport?** chôo-ay pah pŏm (chún) bpai têe sa-năhm bin nòy dâi mái?; **do you take credit cards?** rúp kray-dìt kaht rĕu bplào?; **OK, I'll take it** oh kay, pŏm (chún) ao; **how long does it take?** chái way-lah nahn tâo-rài?; **it'll take 2 hours** chái way-lah sŏrng chôo-a mohng; **is this seat taken?** têe nêe wâhng mái?; **I can't take too much sun** sôo dàirt jùt mâi wăi; **to take away** (*hamburger etc*) ao ... bpai dôo-ay; **will you take this back, it's broken** ja rúp keun mái? mun

dtàirk; **could you take it in at the side?** (*dress, jacket*) ao kâhng kâhng kâo èek; **when does the plane take off?** krêu-ung bin òrk gèe mohng?; **can you take a little off the top?** (*to hairdresser*) dtùt dtrong glahng òrk nòy nèung

talcum powder bpâirng

talk (*verb*) pôot

tall (*person, building*) sŏong

tampax (*tm*) koh-ték

tampons koh-ték

tan (*noun*) klúm; **I want to get a good tan** pŏm (chún) yàhk ja hâi pĕw klúm

tank (*of car*) tŭng núm mun

tap (*for water*) górk náhm

tape (*for cassette, sticky*) táyp

tape measure săi wút

tape recorder krêu-ung bun-téuk sĕe-ung

taste (*noun*) rót; (*verb*) chim; **can I taste it?** kŏr lorng chim nòy, dâi mái?; **it has a peculiar taste** mee rót bplàirk; **it tastes very nice** a-ròy mâhk; **it tastes revolting** mâi a-ròy ler-ee

tax pah-sĕe

Tax Department grom sŭn-pah-gorn

taxi táirk-sêe; **will you get me a taxi?** chôo-ay rêe-uk táirk-sêe hâi nòy, dâi mái?

taxi-driver kon kùp táirk-sêe

taxi rank, taxi stand têe jòrt rót táirk-sêe

tea (*drink*) núm chah; **tea for two please** kŏr núm chah sŏrng têe; **could I have a cup of tea?** kŏr núm chah tôo-ay nèung dâi mái?

teabag chah-tŏong

teach: could you teach me? chôo-ay sŏrn hâi pŏm (chún) nòy, dâi mái; **could you teach me Thai?** chôo-ay sŏrn pah-sǎh tai hâi pŏm (chún) nòy, dâi mái?

teacher (*school*) kroo; (*college*) ah-jahn

teak mái sùk

teak forest bpàh mái sùk

team teem

teapot gah núm chah

tea towel pâh chét jahn

teenager dèk wai rôon

teetotal: he's teetotal káo mâi gin lâo

telegram toh-ra-lâyk; **I want to send a telegram** pŏm (chún) yàhk ja sòng toh-ra-lâyk

telephone toh-ra-sùp; **can I make a telephone call?** pŏm (chún) kŏr toh-ra-sùp nòy, dâi mái?; **could you talk to him for me on the telephone?** chôo-ay pôot gùp káo tairn pŏm (chún) tahng toh-ra-sùp, dâi mái?

telephone box/booth dtôo toh-ra-sùp

telephone directory sa-mòot mǎi-lâyk toh-ra-sùp

telephone number ber toh-ra-sùp; **what's your telephone number?** toh-ra-sùp koon ber a-rai?

telephoto lens layn tay-lay-foh-dtôh

television toh-ra-tút; **I'd like to watch television** pŏm (chún) yàhk ja doo toh-ra-tút; **is the match on television?** gahn kàirng kŭn nêe tài tôrt tee wee rĕu bplào?

tell: could you tell him ...? chôo-ay

bòrk káo wâh ... nòy, dâi mái?

temperature (*weather*) oon-na-ha-poom; (*fever*) kâi; **he has a temperature** káo bpen kâi

temple (*religious*) wút

temporary chôo-a krao

tenant (*of apartment*) kon châo

tennis ten-nít

tennis ball lôok ten-nít

tennis court sa-nǎhm ten-nít; **can we use the tennis court?** kŏr chái sa-nǎhm ten-nít, dâi mái?

tennis racket mái dtee ten-nít

tent tén

term (*at university, school*) term

terminus (*rail*) sa-tǎh-nee

terrace ra-bee-ung; **on the terrace** bon ra-bee-ung

terrible (*weather, food, accent*) yâir mâhk

terrific (*weather, food, teacher*) yôrt yêe-um

testicle gra-bpòhk

Thai (*adjective*) tai; (*language*) pah-sǎh tai; **a Thai/the Thais** kon tai

Thailand (*formal word*) bpra-tâyt tai; (*informal word*) meu-ung tai

than gwàh; **smaller than ...** lék gwàh ...

thanks, thank you kòrp-koon; **thank you very much** kòrp-koon mâhk; **thank you for everything** kòrp-koon sŭm-rùp tóok tóok yàhng; **no thanks** mâi ao kòrp-koon

that: that woman pôo-yǐng kon nún; **that man** pôo-chai kon nún; **that one** un nún; **I hope that ...** pŏm (chún) wǔng wâh ...; **that's perfect** yôrt yêe-um jing jing; **that's strange** bplàirk ná; **is that ...?** ... châi mâi?; **that's it** (*that's right*) châi láir-o; **is it that expensive?** pairng ka-nàht nún chee-o rĕu?

the *see page 95*

theater, theatre rohng la-korn; **National Theatre** rohng la-korn hàirng châht

their kŏrng káo; **their house** bâhn kŏrng káo; *see page 100*

theirs kŏrng káo; *see page 102*

them káo; **for them** sŭm-rùp káo; **with them** gùp káo; **I gave it to them** pŏm (chún) hâi káo bpai; **who? — them** krai? — pôo-uk káo; *see page 101*

then (*after that*) lŭng jàhk nún; (*at that time*) way-lah-nún; (*in that case*) tâh yàhng nún

there têe-nûn; **over there** têe-nôhn; **up there** kâhng bon nún; **is there ...?** mee ... mái?; **are there ...?** mee ... mái?; **there is ...** mee ...; **there are ...** mee ...; **there you are** (*giving something*) nêe krúp (kâ)

thermal spring núm póo rórn

thermometer krêu-ung wút oon-na-ha-poom

thermos flask gra-dtìk núm rórn

these pôo-uk née; **can I have these?** kŏr pôo-uk née dâi mái?

they (*people*) káo; (*things*) mun; **are they ready?** prórm láir-o rěu yung?; **are they coming?** káo ja mah mái? *see page 101*

thick năk; (*stupid*) ngôh

thief ka-moy-ee

thigh nôrng

thin bahng

thing kŏrng; **have you seen my things?** koon hěn kŏrng kŏrng pŏm (chún) mái?; **first thing in the morning** prôong née cháo dtròo

think kít; **what do you think?** koon kít wâh yung-ngai?; **I think so** pŏm (chún) kít wâh yung-ngún; **I don't think so** pŏm (chún) kít wâh kong mâi; **I'll think about it** pŏm (chún) ja lorng kít doo gòrn

third-class chún săhm

third party insurance bpra-gun sŭm-rùp bòok-kon têe săhm

thirsty: I'm thirsty pŏm (chún) hěw náhm; **are you thirsty?** hěw náhm mái?

this: this hotel rohng rairm née; **this street** ta-nŏn née; **this one** un née; **this is my wife** nêe pun-ra-yah kŏrng pŏm; **this is my favo(u)rite**

restaurant nêe ráhn ah-hăhn têe pŏm chôrp mâhk têe sòot; **is this yours?** un née kŏrng koon rěu bplào?

those pôo-uk nún; **not these, those** mâi châi pôo-uk née, pôo-uk nún

thread (*noun*) sên dâi

throat kor hŏy

throat lozenges yah om gâir kor jèp

throttle (*on motorbike*) kun rêng núm mun

through pàhn; **does it go through Korat?** pàhn koh-râht rěu bplào?; **Monday through Friday** wun jun těung wun sòok; **straight through the city centre** pàhn jai glahng meu-ung

throughout dta-lòrt; **throughout the time I was there** dta-lòrt way-lah têe pŏm (chún) yòo têe-nûn

through train rót fai rôrt dee-o

throw (*verb*) kwâhng; **don't throw it away** yàh tíng ná; **I'm going to throw up** pŏm (chún) róo-sèuk ja ah-jee-un

thumb néw hŏo-a mâir meu

thumbtack bpék

thunder (*noun*) fáh rórng

thunderstorm pah-yóo fŏn

Thursday wun pá-réu-hùt

ticket (*for bus, train, plane, cinema, cloakroom*) dtŏo-a

ticket office (*bus, rail*) têe jum-nài dtŏo-a

tie (*noun: around neck*) nék-tai

tight (*clothes etc*) kúp; **the waist is too tight** ay-o kúp gern bpai

tights tái

time way-lah; (*occasion*) krúng; **what's the time?** gèe mohng láir-o?; **at what time do you close?** koon bpìt gèe mohng?; **there's not much time** lěu-a way-lah mâi mâhk; **for the time being** dtorn née; **from time to time** bpen krúng bpen krao; **right on time** dtrong way-lah bpěng ler-ee; **this time** krúng née; **last time** krúng têe láir-o; **next time** krúng nâh; **four times** sèe krúng; **have a**

good time! kŏr hâi sa-nòok ná; *see page 112*

timetable dtah-rahng way-lah

tin (*can*) gra-bpŏrng

tinfoil gra-dàht a-loo-mi-nee-um

tinned milk nom gra-bpŏrng

tin-opener têe bpèrt gra-bpŏrng

tint (*verb: hair*) chairm sĕe

tiny lék; **a tiny bit** nít nèung

tip (*to waiter etc*) ngern típ; **does that include the tip?** rôo-um kâh típ rĕu bplào?

tire (*for car*) yahng rót

tired nèu-ay; **I'm tired** pŏm (chún) nèu-ay

tiring nâh nèu-ay nài

tissues pâh nèu-ay chét meu

to: to England bpai ung-grìt; **to London** bpai lorn-dorn; **to the airport** bpai sa-nǎhm bin; *see page 112*

toast (*bread*) ka-nŏm bpung bpîng; (*drinking*) dèum oo-ay porn

toasted bananas glôo-ay bpîng

tobacco yah sòop

tobacconist, tobacco store ráhn kǎi yah sòop

today wun-née; **today week** wun-née ah-tít nâh

toe néw táo

toffee tórp-fêe

together dôo-ay gun; **we're together** rao mah dôo-ay gun; **can we pay together?** jài roo-um gun dâi mái?

toilet hôrng náhm; **where's the toilet?** hôrng náhm yòo têe nǎi?; **I have to go to the toilet** pŏm (chún) dtôrng bpai hôrng náhm; **she's in the toilet** káo yòo nai hôrng náhm

toilet paper gra-dàht chum-rá

toilet water núm hŏrm

toll (*for motorway, bridge etc*) kâh pàhn tahng

tomato ma-kĕu-a tâyt

tomato juice núm ma-kĕu-a tâyt

tomato ketchup sórt ma-kĕu-a tâyt

tomorrow prôong née; **tomorrow morning** cháo prôong née; **tomorrow afternoon** bài prôong née; **tomorrow evening** yen prôong

née; **the day after tomorrow** ma-reun-née; **see you tomorrow** jer gun prôong née

ton dtun; *see page 114*

toner (*cosmetic*) 'toner'

tongue lín

tonic (water) núm toh-ník

tonight keun née; **not tonight** mâi ao keun née; **it's not tonight** mâi châi keun née

tonsillitis dtòrm torn-sin ùk-sàyp

tonsils dtòm torn-sin

too (*excessively*) ... gern bpai; (*also*) ... dôo-ay; **too much** mâhk gern bpai; **I'd like to go too** pŏm (chún) yàhk bpai dôo-ay; **me too** pŏm (chún) gôr mĕu-un gun; **I'm not feeling too good** pŏm (chún) róo-sèuk mâi kôy sa-bai

tooth fun

toothache bpòot-ut fun

toothbrush bprairng sĕe fun

toothpaste yah sĕe fun

top: on top of ... yòo bon ...; **on top of the car** yòo bon lŭng-kah rót; **on the top floor** chún bon; **at the top** yòo kâhng bon; **at the top of the hill** yòo bon yôrt kǎo; **top quality** koon-na-pâhp yôrt yêe-um; **bikini top** sêu-a bpi-gee-nêe

topless bpleu-ay òk

torch fai chǎi

tortoise dtào

total (*noun*) roo-um yôrt

touch (*verb*) dtàir-dtôrng; **let's keep in touch** dtôrng sòng kào tĕung gun bâhng ná

tough (*meat*) nĕe-o; **tough luck!** chôhk rái!

tour (*noun*) rai-gahn num têe-o; **is there a tour of ...?** mee rai-gahn num têe-o bpai ... mái?

tour guide (*book*) núng-sĕu num têe-o; (*person*) múk-koo-tàyt

tourist núk tôrng têe-o

tourist information office sŭm-núk kào sǎhn núk tôrng têe-o

touristy làirng núk tôrng têe-o; **somewhere not so touristy** têe nǎi gôr dâi têe mâi châi làirng núk tôrng têe-o

tour operator pôo-jùt bor-ri-gahn num têe-o

tow: can you give me a tow? chôo-ay lâhk nòy, dâi mái?

toward(s) sòo; **toward(s) Hua Hin** bpai sòo hŏo-a hĭn

towel pâh chét dtoo-a

town meu-ung; **in town** nai meu-ung; **which bus goes into town?** rót săi năi kâo meu-ung?; **we're staying just out of town** rao yòo nôrk meu-ung bpai nòy

town hall tâyt-sa-bahn

tow rope chêu-uk lâhk

toy kŏrng lên

track suit chóot worm

trade (*commerce*) gahn káh; (*occupation*) káh kăi

tradition ka-nòp-tum-nee-um; **Thai tradition(s)** ka-nòp-tum-nee-um tai

traditional: a traditional Thai meal ah-hăhn bàirp tai táir

traffic ja-rah-jorn

traffic circle wong wee-un

traffic cop dtum-ròo-ut ja-rah-jorn

traffic jam rót dtìt

traffic light(s) fai sŭn-yahn ja-rah-jorn

trailer (*for carrying tent etc*) rót pôo-ung

train rót fai; **when's the next train to ...?** rót fai bpai ... ka-boo-un nâh òrk gèe mohng?; **by train** doy-ee rót fai

trainers (*shoes*) rorng táo wîng

train station sa-tăhn-nee rót fai

tramp (*person*) kon jorn-jùt

tranquillizers yah glòrm bpra-sàht

transfer desk 'transfer desk'

transformer (*electrical*) krêu-ung bplairng fai

transistor (*radio*) wít-ta-yóo trahn-sít-sa-dter

translate bplair; **could you translate that?** chôo-ay bplair hâi nòy, dâi mái?

translation gahn bplair

translator pôo bplair

transmission (*of car*) 'transmission'

travel gahn dern tahng; **we're travel(l)ing around** rao dern tahng bpai rêu-ay rêu-ay

travel agent 'travel agent'

travel(l)er pôo dern tahng

traveller's cheque, traveler's check chék dern tahng

tray tàht

tree dtôn mái

tremendous wí-sàyt

trendy (*person, clothes, restaurant*) tun sa-măi

tricky (*difficult*) lum-bàhk

trim: just a trim please (*to hairdresser*) chôo-ay klìp tâo-nún krúp (kâ)

trip: I'd like to go on a trip to ... pŏm (chún) yàhk ja bpai têe-o ...; **have a good trip** kŏr hâi têe-o sa-nòok ná; **we made a week-long trip to the north** rao bpai têe-o pâhk nĕu-a ah-tít nèung

tripod (*for camera*) kăh dtûng glôrng tài rôop

trishaw rót săhm lór

tropical (*heat, climate*) rórn jùt

trouble (*noun*) bpun-hăh; **I'm having trouble with ...** pŏm (chún) mee bpun-hăh gùp ...; **sorry to trouble you** kŏr-tôht têe róp-goo-un

trousers gahng-gayng

trouser suit chóot sêu-a gahng-gayng

truck rót bun-tóok

truck driver kon kùp rót bun-tóok

true jing; **that's not true** mâi jing

trunk (*of car*) gra-bprohng tái; (*for belongings: big case*); gra-bpăo dern tahng; (*of elephant*) ngoo-ung cháhng

trunks (*swimming*) gahng-gayng wâi náhm

truth kwahm jing; **it's the truth** bpen kwahm jing

try (*perservere*) pa-ya-yahm; (*try out, test*) lorng; **please try** (*make the effort*) pa-yah-yahm nòy ná; **will you try for me?** pa-yah-yahm pêu-a pŏm (chún) ja dâi mái?; **I've never tried it** (*food etc*) pŏm (chún) mâi ker-ee

lorng mah gòrn; **can I have a try?**
(*food, at doing something*) kǒr lorng
nòy, dâi mái?; **may I try it on?**
(*clothes*) kǒr lorng sài doo nòy, dâi
mái?
T-shirt sêu-a yêut
tube (*for tyre*) yahng nai
Tuesday wun ung-kahn
tuition: I'd like tuition pǒm (chún)
yàhk ree-un
tune (*noun*) tum-norng
tunnel oo-mohng
turn: it's my turn now tĕung tee
kǒrng pǒm (chún) láir-o; **turn left**
lée-o sái; **where do we turn off?** rao
ja lée-o tée nǎi?; **can you turn the
air-conditioning on?** chôo-ay bpèrt
krêu-ung bprùp ah-gàht nòy, dâi
mái?; **can you turn the air-
conditioning off?** chôo-ay bpìt
krêu-ung bprùp ah-gàht nòy, dâi

mái?; **he didn't turn up** káo mâi dâi
mah
turning (*in road*) tahng lée-o
turtle dtào
tusk (*of elephant*) ngah cháhng
TV tee-wee
tweezers bpàhk kêep
twice sǒrng krúng; **twice as much**
mâhk sǒrng tâo
twin beds dtee-ung kôo
twin room hôrng kôo
twins fàirt
twist: I've twisted my ankle kôr táo
pǒm (chún) plík
type (*noun*) bàirp; **a different type of
...** ... èek bàirp nèung
typewriter krêu-ung pim dèet
typhoid kâi tai-foy
typical (*dish etc*) bàirp cha-bùp; **that's
typical!** bpen yàhng née sa-měr!
tyre yahng rót

U

ugly (*person, building*) nâh glèe-ut
ulcer plǎir gra-pór
Ulster 'Ulster'
umbrella rôm
uncle (*older brother of father or mother*)
loong; (*younger brother of father*) ah;
(*younger brother of mother*) náh
uncomfortable (*chair etc*) mâi sa-bai
unconscious mòt sa-dtì
under (*spatially*) dtâi; (*less than*) dtùm
gwàh
underdone (*meat*) sòok-sòok dìp-dìp
underpants gahng-gayng nai
undershirt sêu-a chún nai
understand: I don't understand pǒm
(chún) mâi kâo jai; **I understand**
pǒm (chún) kâo jai; **do you understand?** kâo jai mái?
underwear sêu-a pâh chún nai

undo (*clothes*) gâir
undress tòrt sêu-a
uneatable: it's uneatable gin mâi
long
unemployed wâhng ngahn
unfair: that's unfair mâi yóot-dti-tum
unfortunately chôhk rái
unfriendly mâi bpen mít
unhappy mâi sa-bai jai
unhealthy (*person*) sòok-a-pâhp mâi
dee; (*climate etc*) mâi tòok sòok-a-
pâhp
uniform (*noun*) krêu-ung bàirp
United States sa-hà-rút a-may-ri-gah;
in the United States nai sa-hà-rút a-
may-ri-gah
university ma-hǎh-wít-ta-yah-lai
unlimited mileage (*on hire car*) mâi
jum-gùt ra-yá tahng

unlock kǎi goon-jair; **the door was unlocked** bpra-dtoo mâi bpìt goon-jair

unpack gâir hòr

unpleasant (*person, taste*) nâh rung-gèe-ut

unpronounceable pôot mâi dâi

untie gâir

until jon; **until we meet again** (*said as parting words*) jon gwàh rao ja póp gun èek; **I'm staying until Wednesday** pǒm (chún) yòo jon tĕung wun póot

unusual pìt tum-ma-dah

up kêun; **further up the road** ler-ee ta-nǒn bpai èek; **up there** yòo bon nún; **he's not up yet** (*not out of bed*) káo yung mâi dtèun; **what's up?** (*what's wrong?*) bpen a-rai?

up-country (*outside Bangkok*) dtàhng jung-wùt

upmarket (*restaurant, hotel, goods etc*) rǒo-rǎh

upset stomach tórng sĕe-a

upside down kwûm

upstairs kâhng bon

urgent dòo-un; **it's very urgent** dòo-un mâhk

urinary tract infection rôhk tahng dern bpùt-sǎh-wá ùk-sàyp

us rao; **with us** gùp rao; **for us** sǔm-rùp rao; *see page 101*

use (*verb*) chái; **may I use ...?** kǒr chái ... nòy, dâi mái?

used: I used to swim a lot pǒm ker-ee wâi náhm mâhk mâhk; **when I get used to the heat** way-lah pǒm (chún) chin gùp ah-gàht

useful mee bpra-yòht

usual tum-ma-dah; **as usual** dtahm tum-ma-dah

usually tum-ma-dah

V

vacancy: do you have any vacancies? (*hotel*) mee hôrng wâhng mái?

vacation wun yòot; **we're here on vacation** rao mah têe-o púk-porn wun yòot

vaccination chèet wúk-seen

vacuum cleaner krêu-ung dòot fòon

vacuum flask gra-dtìk núm rórn

vagina chôrng klôrt

valid (*ticket etc*) chái dâi; **how long is it valid for?** chái dâi tĕung mêu-a rài?

valley hòop kǎo

valuable (*adjective*) mee kâh

valuables kâo kǒrng mee kâh; **can I leave my valuables here?** ao kâo kǒrng tíng wái têe nêe, dâi mái?

value (*noun*) kâh

van rót dtôo

vanilla wá-née-lah; **a vanilla ice cream** ay kreem wá-née-lah

varicose veins sên loh-hìt porng

various dtàhng dtàhng

vary: it varies láir-o dtàir

vase jair-gun

VD wee dee; (*contracted by men*) rôhk pôo-yǐng; (*contracted by women*) rôhk boo-ròot

vegetables pùk

vegetarian mâi gin néu-a; **I'm a vegetarian** pǒm (chún) bpen kon mâi gin néu-a

velvet gum-ma-yèe

vending machine dtôo

ventilator krêu-ung tài tay ah-gàht

very mâhk; **very hot** rórn mâhk; **I like it very much** pǒm (chún) chôrp

mâhk; **just a very little Thai** pah-
săh tai nít dee-o; **just a very little
for me** kŏr nít dee-o tâo-nún
vest (*under shirt*) sêu-a glâhm; (*waistcoat*) sêu-a gúk
via pàhn; **via Korat** pàhn koh-râht
vicinity bor-ri-wayn
video (*noun: film*) wee-dee-oh; (*recorder*) krêu-ung wee-dee-oh
view wew; **what a superb view!** wew
sŏo-ay mâhk!
viewfinder (*of camera*) têe jùt pâhp
village mòo-bâhn
villager chao bâhn
village headman pôo-yài bâhn

vinegar núm sôm
visa wee-sâh
visibility: the visibility was poor
morng mâi kôy hĕn
visit (*places*) têe-o; (*people*) yêe-um; **I'd
like to visit ...** pŏm (chún) yàhk ja
bpai têe-o/yêe-um ...; **come and visit
us** mah yêe-um rao ná
vital: it's vital that ... sŭm-kun mâhk
têe ja dtôrng ...
vitamins wi-dtah-min
vodka word-kâh
voice sĕe-ung
voltage rairng fai fáh
vomit ah-jee-un

wafer (*with ice cream*) 'wafer'
waist ay-o
waistcoat sêu-a gúk
wait ror; **wait for me** ror pŏm (chún)
nòy ná; **don't wait for me** mâi
dtôrng ror pŏm (chún) ná; **it was
worth waiting for** kóom kâh têe
ror; **I'll wait until my wife comes**
pŏm ja ror jon gwàh pun-ra-yah ja
mah; **I'll wait a little longer** pŏm
(chún) ja ror èek súk krôo; **can you
do it while I wait?** pŏm (chún) ror
ao dâi mái?
waiter kon sèrp; **waiter!** koon krúp
(kâ)!
waiting room hôrng púk
waitress kon sèrp yĭng; **waitress!**
koon krúp (kâ)!
wake: will you wake me up at 6.30?
chôo-ay bplòok pŏm (chún) way-lah
hòk mohng krêung dâi mái?
Wales 'Wales'
walk: let's walk there dern bpai tèr;
is it possible to walk there? dern
bpai dâi mái?; **I'll walk back** pŏm

(chún) ja dern glùp; **is it a long
walk?** dern glai mái?; **it's only a
short walk** dern mâi glai; **I'm going
out for a walk** pŏm (chún) ja òrk
bpai dern lên; **let's take a walk
around town** bpai dern lên rôrp
rôrp meu-ung gun tèr
walking: I want to do some walking
pŏm (chún) yàhk ja bpai dern bâhng
walking boots rórng táo dern
walking stick mái táo
walkman (*tm*) 'walkman'
wall (*inside*) făh; (*outside*) gum-pairng
wallet gra-bpăo sa-dtung
**wander: I like just wandering
around** pŏm (chún) chôrp dern lên
rêu-ay bpèu-ay bpai
want: I want a ... pŏm (chún) yàhk
dâi ...; **I don't want any ...** pŏm
(chún) mâi yàhk dâi ...; **I want to ...**
pŏm (chún) yàhk ja ...; **I want to go
home** pŏm (chún) yàhk ja glùp
bâhn; **is he coming with us? — no,
he doesn't want to** káo ja mah dôo-
ay rĕu bplào? — káo mâi yàhk mah;

he wants to ... káo yàhk ja ...; **what
do you want?** koon dtôrng-gahn a-
rai?

war sŏng-krahm

ward (*in hospital*) hŏr pôo bpòo-ay

warm: it's so warm today wun née
rórn jung; **I'm so warm** pŏm (chún)
rórn jung

warning (*noun*) kum dteu-un

was: it was ... bpen ...; *see page 98*

wash (*verb*) láhng; **to wash clothes**
súk pâh; **to wash one's hair** sà pŏm;
I need a wash pŏm (chún) dtôrng-
gahn láhng meu láhng nâh; **can you
wash the car?** láhng rót hâi nòy dâi
mái?; **can you wash these clothes?**
súk pâh née hâi nòy dâi mái?; **it'll
wash off** súk òrk dâi; **I want to
wash my hair** pŏm (chún) yàhk ja sà
pŏm

washcloth pâh láhng nâh

washer (*for bolt etc*) wong-wăirn

washhand basin àhng láhng nâh

washing (*clothes*): **where can I do my
washing?** pŏm (chún) súk pâh dâi
têe năi?; **where can I hang my
washing?** pŏm (chún) dtàhk pâh dâi
têe năi?; **can you do my washing
for me?** súk pâh hâi dâi mái?

washing machine krêu-ung súk pâh

washing powder pŏng súk fôrk

washing-up: I'll do the washing-up
pŏm (chún) ja láhng jahn ayng

washing-up liquid núm yah láhng
jahn

wasp dtairn

waste: it's a waste of time sěe-a way-
lah; **it's a waste of money** sěe-a
ngern bplào bplào

wasteful: that's wasteful sěe-a kŏrng

wastepaper basket dta-gràh ka-yà

wat (*Thai temple*) wút

watch (*wrist-*) nah-li-gah kôr meu;
will you watch my things for me?
chôo-ay fâo kŏrng hâi nòy dâi mái?;
I'll just watch pŏm (chún) kŏr doo
tâo-nún; **watch out!** ra-wung ná!

watch strap săi nah-li-gah

water náhm; **may I have some water?**
kŏr náhm nòy dâi mái?

water buffalo kwai

watercolo(u)r (*painting*) pâhp sěe
náhm

waterfall núm dtòk

water melon dtairng moh

waterproof (*adjective*) gun náhm

waterski: I'd like to learn to waterski
pŏm (chún) yàhk ja ree-un lên sa-
gee náhm

waterskiing sa-gee náhm

water sports gee-lah náhm

water wings yahng hùt wâi náhm

wave (*in sea*) klêun

way: which way is it? bpai tahng
năi?; **it's this way** bpai tahng née;
it's that way bpai tahng nôhn; **could
you tell me the way to ...?** chôo-ay
bòrk tahng bpai ... hâi nòy, dâi
mái?; **is it on the way to Bangkok?**
tahng bpai groong-tâyp rĕu bplào?;
you're blocking the way koon
kwăhng tahng; **is it a long way to
...?** bpai ... glai mái?; **would you
show me the way to do it?** chôo-ay
sa-dairng wí-tee tum hâi nòy dâi
mái?; **do it this way** tum yung née;
no way! mâi mee tahng!

we rao; *see page 101*

weak (*person*) òrn-air; (*drink*) òrn

wealthy rûm roo-ay

weather ah-gàht; **what foul weather!**
ah-gàht yâir jung!; **what beautiful
weather!** ah-gàht dee jung ler-ee!

weather forecast rai-ngahn ah-gàht

wedding pi-tee dtàirng ngahn

wedding anniversary cha-lŏrng króp
rôrp wun dtàirng ngahn

wedding ring wăirn dtàirng ngahn

Wednesday wun póot

week ah-tít; **a week (from) today** èek
ah-tít nèung jàhk wun née bpai; **a
week (from) tomorrow** èek ah-tít
nèung jàhk prôong née bpai; **Monday week** wun jun nâh

weekend wun săo ah-tít; **at/on the
weekend** wun săo ah-tít

weight núm-nùk; **I want to lose
weight** pŏm (chún) yàhk lót núm-

nùk

weight limit (*for baggage, bridge*) núm-nùk jum-gùt

weird (*person, custom, thing to happen*) bplàirk

welcome: welcome to ... ... kŏr dtôrn rúp; **you're welcome** (*don't mention it*) mâi bpen rai

well: I don't feel well pŏm (chún) róo-sèuk mâi kôy sa-bai; **I haven't been very well** pŏm (chún) mâi kôy sa-bai; **she's not well** káo mâi sa-bai; **how are you — very well, thanks** bpen yung-ngai bâhng? — sa-bai dee kòrp-kOOn; **you speak English very well** kOOn pôot pah-săh ung-grìt dâi dee mâhk; **me as well** pŏm (chún) gôr mĕu-un gun; **well done!** dee mâhk!; **well well!** (*surprise*) măir!

well-done (*meat*) sòok sòok

wellingtons rorng táo bóot

Welsh jàhk meu-ung 'Wales'

were: they were ... bpen ... *see page 98*

west dta-wun dtòk; **to the west** tahng tít dta-wun dtòk

West Indian (*person*) chao mòo gòr in-dee-a dta-wun dtòk

West Indies mòo gòr in-dee-a dta-wun dtòk

wet bpèe-uk; **it's all wet** bpèe-uk mòt; **it's been wet all week** fŏn dtòk dta-lòrt ah-tít

wet suit (*for diving etc*) chóot dum náhm

what? a-rai?; **what's that?** nûn a-rai?; **what is he saying?** káo pôot wâh yung-ngai?; **I don't know what to do** pŏm (chún) mâi sâhp wâh ja tum yung-ngai; **what a view!** wew sŏo-ay jung ler-ee!

wheel lór

wheelchair rót kĕn sŭm-rùp kon bpòo-ay

when? mêu-a rài?; **when we get back here/there** mêu-a rao glùp mah/bpai; **when we got back here/there** mêu-a rao glùp mah/bpai láir-o

where? têe năi?; **where is ...?** ... yòo

têe năi?; **I don't know where he is** pŏm (chún) mâi sâhp wâh káo yòo têe năi; **that's where I left it** pŏm (chún) tíng wái têe nûn

which: which bus? rót may săi năi?; **which one?** un năi?; **which is yours?** un năi kŏrng kOOn?; **I forget which it was** pŏm (chún) leum bpai láir-o wâh un năi; **the one which ...** un têe ...

while (*conjunction*) ka-nà têe; **while I'm here** ka-nà têe pŏm (chún) yòo têe nêe

whisky lâo wít-sa-gêe; **Mekhong whisky** (*tm*) lâo mâir-kŏhng

whisper (*verb*) gra-síp

white sĕe kăo

white wine lâo wai kăo

who? krai?; **who was that?** nûn krai?; **the man who ...** kon têe ...

whole: the whole week dta-lòrt ah-tít; **two whole days** dta-lòrt sŏrng wun; **the whole lot** túng mòt

whooping cough ai gron

whose: whose is this? nêe kŏrng krai?

why? tum-mai?; **that's why it's not working** prór yung ngún mun tĕung sĕe-a

wide gwâhng

wide-angle lens layn mOOm gwâhng

widow mâir mâi

widower pôr mâi

wife: my wife pun-ra-yah kŏrng pŏm

wig pŏm bplorm

will: will you ask him? chôo-ay tăhm káo nòy dâi mái?; *see page 103*

win (*verb*) cha-ná; **who won?** krai cha-ná?

wind (*noun*) lom

window nâh-dtàhng; **near the window** glâi nâh-dtàhng; **in the window** (*of shop*) têe nâh-dtàhng

window seat têe nûng dtìt nâh-dtàhng

windscreen, windshield gra-jòk nâh rót yon

windscreen wipers, windshield wipers têe bpùt núm fŏn

windy lom rairng; **it's so windy** lom rairng mâhk

wine lâo wai; **can we have some more wine?** kŏr wai èek dâi mái?

wine glass gâir-o wai

wine list rai-gahn lâo wai

wing (*of plane, bird, car*) bpèek

winter nâh nǎo; **in the winter** nai nâh nǎo

winter holiday wun yòot púk pòrn nâh nǎo

wire sên lôo-ut; (*electrical*) sǎi fai fáh

wireless wít-ta-yóo

wiring dern sǎi

wish: best wishes dôo-ay kwahm bpràht-ta-nǎh dee

with gùp; **I'm staying with ...** pǒm (chún) púk yòo gùp ...

without: without milk/sugar mâi sài nom/num dtahn

witness pa-yahn; **will you be a witness for me?** chôo-ay bpen pa-yahn hâi pǒm (chún) dâi mái?

witty chèe-up lǎirm

wobble: it wobbles (*wheel*) wôrk wâirk

woman pôo-yǐng

women pôo-yǐng

wonderful (*holiday, meal, weather, person*) yôrt yêe-um

won't: it won't start mâi yorm dtìt; *see page 108*

wood (*material*) mái; **made of wood** tum dôo-ay mái

woods (*forest*) bpàh

wool kǒn sùt

word kum; **you have my word** (*I promise*) pǒm (chún) kǒr sǔn-yah

work (*verb*) tum ngahn; (*noun*) ngahn; **how does it work?** chái yung-ngai?; **it's not working** mun sěe-a; **I work in an office** pǒm (chún) tum ngahn nai sǔm-núk ngahn; **do you have any work for me?** mee ngahn hâi pǒm (chún) tum mái?; **when do you finish work?** koon lêrk ngahn mêu-a rài?

work permit bai a-nóo-yâht tum ngahn

world lôhk; **all over the world** tôo-a lôhk

worn-out (*person*) nèu-ay nài; (*shoes, clothes*) gào

worry (*verb*) bpen hòo-ung; **I'm worried about her** pǒm (chún) bpen hòo-ung káo; **don't worry** mâi dtôrng bpen hòo-ung

worse: it's worse yâir long; **it's getting worse** gum-lung yâir long tóok tee

worst yâir têe sòot

worth: it's not worth 500 baht mâi mee kâh těung hâh róy bàht; **it's worth more than that** mee kâh mâhk gwàh nún; **is it worth a visit?** nâh têe-o mái?

would: would you give this to ...? chôo-ay ao nêe bpai hâi ... dâi mái?; **what would you do?** koon ja tum yung-ngai?

wound (*noun*) bàht plǎir

wrap: could you wrap it up? chôo-ay hòr hâi nòy, dâi mái?

wrapping krêu-ung hòr

wrapping paper gra-dàht hòr kǒrng kwǔn

wrench (*tool*) goon-jair bpàhk dtai

wrist kôr-meu

write kěe-un; **could you write it down?** chôo-ay kěe-un long hâi nòy, dâi mái?; **how do you write it?** kěe-un yung-ngai?; **I'll write to you** pǒm (chún) ja kěe-un těung koon; **I wrote to you last month** pǒm (chún) kěe-un těung koon mêu-a deu-un têe láir-o

write-off: it's a write-off (*car etc*) chái gahn mâi dâi

writer núk kěe-un

writing (*act*) gahn kěe-un; **Thai writing** (*act*) gahn kěe-un pah-sǎh tai; (*script*) dtoo-a ùk-sǒrn tai; **I can't read Thai writing** pǒm (chún) àhn pah-sǎh tai mâi òrk

writing paper gra-dàht kěe-un jòt-mǎi

wrong pìt; **you're wrong** koon pìt; **the bill's wrong** kít bin pìt; **sorry, wrong number** kǒr-tôht dtòr ber pìt;

I'm on the wrong train pŏm (chún) kêun rót fai pìt; **I went to the wrong room** pŏm (chún) kâo hôrng pìt; **that's the wrong key** nûn gOOn-jair pìt hôrng; **there's some-** thing wrong with ... ... mee a-rai pìt; **what's wrong?** bpen a-rai?; **what's wrong with it?** mun pìt yung-ngai?

X-ray 'X-ray'

xylophone ra-nâht

yacht reu-a yórt
yacht club 'yacht club'
yard: in the yard nai bor-ri-wayn bâhn; *see page 113*
year bpee
yellow sĕe lĕu-ung
yellow pages sa-mòot yay-loh páyt
yes: is this yours? — **yes** nêe kŏrng kOOn châi mái? — châi; **this one?** — **yes** un née lĕr? — krúp (kâ); **would you like some more?** — **yes** ao èek mái? — ao; **are you going?** — **yes** bpai rĕu bplào? — bpai; (*answering phone*) krúp (kâ); *see page 105*
yesterday mêu-a wahn née; **yesterday morning** cháo wahn née; **yesterday afternoon** bài wahn née; **the day**

before yesterday wahn seun née
yet: has it arrived yet? mah tĕung rĕu yung?; **not yet** yung
yobbo jík-gŏh
yog(h)urt 'yoghurt'
you (*singular and plural*) (*polite*) kOOn; (*very polite*) tûn; (*familiar*) ter; **this is for you** nêe sŭm-rùp kOOn; **with you** gùp kOOn; *see pages 101, 102*
young: a young man nòom; **a young woman** săo; **a young baby** dèk òrn
young people nòom nòom săo săo
your kŏrng kOOn; **your camera** glôrng tài rôop kŏrng kOOn; *see page 100*
yours kŏrng kOOn; *see page 102*

Z

zero sǒon

zip, zipper síp; **could you put a new zip on?** chôo-ay dừt síp mài hâi

dôo-ay dâi mái?

zoo sǒo-un sùt

zoom lens layn soom

Thai-English

LIST OF SUBJECT AREAS

ABBREVIATIONS

ป.อ. *[bprùp ah-gàht]* air-conditioned

ก.ท.ม. *[grOOng-tâyp-ma-hăh-na-korn]* Bangkok

พ.ศ. *[pÓOt-ta-sùk-ga-ràht]* Buddhist Era (B.E.) *(543 years later than A.D.)*

ค.ศ. *[krít-dta-sùk-ga-ràht]* Christian Era (A.D.)

อ. *[um-per]* Amphoe, district

พ.ญ. *[pâirt yĭng]* Dr *(female, medical)*

น.พ. *[nai pâirt]* Dr *(male, medical)*

คร. *[dork-dtêr]* Dr *(non-medical)*

ร.ส.พ. *[rúp sòng sĭn-káh láir pút-sa-dÒO]* Express Transport Organization

ร.พ. *[rohng pa-yah-bahn]* hospital

ช.ม. *[chôo-a mohng]* hours

น. *[nah-li-gah]* Hrs. *(24-hr clock)*

ก.ม. *[gi-loh-mét]* kilometre, kilometer

ช. *[chai]* men

น.ส. *[nahng săo]* Miss

จ. *[jung-wùt]* province

ถ. *[ta-nŏn]* road

ต. *[dtum-bon]* Tambon, sub-district

ร.ฟ.ท. *[rót fai tai]* Thai State Railways/ Railroad Authority

บ.ข.ส. *[bor-ri-sùt kŏn sòng]* Transport Company

ญ. *[yĭng]* women

AIRPORT AND PLANE

ที่ทำการบริษัทการบิน *[têe tum gahn bor-ri-sùt gahn bin]* airline company offices

ท่าอากาศยาน *[tâh ah-gàht-sa-yahn]* airport

ศุลกากร *[sǒOn-la-gah-gorn]* customs

ตรวจคนเข้าเมือง *[dtròo-ut kon kâo meu-ung]* immigration

สอบถาม *[sòrp tǎhm]* information

ฝากกระเป๋า *[fàhk gra-bpǎo]* left luggage, baggage checkroom

ลิฟท์ *[lif]* lift, elevator

จุดนัดพบ *[jòot nút póp]* meeting point

จุดตรวจค้นผู้โดยสาร *[jòot dtròo-ut kón pôo doy-ee sǎhn]* passenger checkpoint

เฉพาะผู้โดยสารและลูกเรือเท่านั้น *[cha-pòr pôo doy-ee sǎhn láir lôok reu-a tâo-nún]* passengers and crew only

ตรวจหนังสือเดินทาง *[dtròo-ut núng-sěu dern tahng]* passport control

ประชาสัมพันธ์ ท่าอากาศยานกรุงเทพ *[bpra-chah sǔm-pun tâh-ah-gàht-sa-yahn grOOng-tâyp]* public relations, Bangkok Airport

ภัตตาคาร *[pút-dtah-kahn]* restaurant

ตรวจสอบบัตรผู้โดยสารและกระเป๋า *[dtròo-ut sòrp bùt pôo doy-ee sǎhn láir gra-bpǎo]* ticket and baggage check

สุขา หญิง-ชาย *[sǒO-kǎh yǐng - chai]* toilets/rest rooms women - men

ผู้มาส่งผู้โดยสาร *[pôo mah sòng pôo doy-ee sǎhn]* visitors

ที่พักผู้มาส่งผู้โดยสาร *[têe púk pôo mah sòng pôo doy-ee sǎhn]* visitors' waiting area

BANKS

บาท *[bàht]* baht *(unit of currency)*

ธนาคาร *[ta-nah-kahn]* bank

ฝากประจำ *[fàhk bpra-jum]* deposit account, savings account

ฝากเงิน *[fàhk ngern]* deposits

แลกเปลี่ยนเงินตราต่างประเทศ *[lâirk bplèe-un ngern dtrah dtàhng bpra-tâyt]* foreign exchange

อัตราแลกเปลี่ยนเงินตราต่างประเทศ *[ùt-dtrah lâirk bplèe-un ngern dtrah dtàhng bpra-tâyt]* foreign exchange rate

สอบถาม *[sòrp tǎhm]* inquiries

เปิดบัญชีใหม่ *[bpèrt bun-chee mài]* new accounts

ถอนเงิน *[tǒrn ngern]* withdrawals

BARS *see* RESTAURANTS
BUS STATION

รถปรับอากาศ *[rót bprùp ah-gàht]* air-conditioned bus

ถึง *[těung]* arrives

ออก *[òrk]* departs

สอบถาม *[sòrp tǎhm]* inquiries

รับฝากของ *[rúp fàhk kǒrng]* left luggage, baggage checkroom

รถธรรมดา *[rót tum-ma-dah]* ordinary bus

ทางเข้าเฉพาะผู้ถือตั๋วโดยสาร *[tahng kâo cha-pòr pôo těu dtǒo-a doy-ee sǎhn]* passengers with tickets only

ห้องพักผู้โดยสาร *[hôrng púk pôo doy-ee sǎhn]* passengers' waiting room

ประชาสัมพันธ์ *[bpra-chah-sǔm-pun]* public relations

ที่จำหน่ายตั๋ว *[têe jum-nài dtǒo-a]* ticket office

กำหนดเวลาเดินรถ *[gum-nòt way-lah dern rót]* timetable, schedule

สุขา หญิง-ชาย *[sǒO-kǎh yǐng - chai]* toilets/rest rooms ladies - men

รถทัวร์ *[rót too-a]* tour bus

CINEMAS

บาท *[... bàht]* ... baht

ถุงละ ... บาท *[tǒOng la ... bàht]* ... baht per bag

ถ้วยละ ... บาท *[tôo-ay la ... bàht]* ... baht per cup

ชิ้นละ ... บาท *[chín la ... bàht]* ... baht per piece

รอบ 17.00 น. *[rôrp 17.00 n(ah-li-gah)]* 5 pm show

เร็ว ๆ นี้ *[ray-o ray-o née]* coming soon

สุขาหญิง *[sÒO-kǎh yǐng]* ladies' toilet/ rest room

ทรงพระเจริญ *[song prá ja-rern]* long live the King!

สุขาชาย *[sÒO-kǎh chai]* men's toilet, men's room

รายการหน้า *[rai-gahn nâh]* next program(me)

อาทิตย์หน้า *[ah-tĭt nâh]* next week

ห้ามสูบบุหรี่ *[hâhm sòop bOO-rèe]* no smoking

ราคา *[rah-kah]* price

ฉายวันนี้ *[chǎi wun née]* showing today

ที่จำหน่ายตั๋ว *[têe jum-nài dtǒo-a]* ticket office

ทางออก *[tahng òrk]* way out

COUNTRIES AND NATIONALITIES

อีก้อ *[ee-gôr]* Akha *(hill tribe)*

อเมริกา *[a-may-ri-gah]* America, American

ออสเตรเลีย *[òrt-sa-dtray-lee-a]* Australia, Australian

พม่า *[pa-mâh]* Burma, Burmese

จีน *[jeen]* China, Chinese

ประเทศ *[bpra-tâyt]* country *(formal word)*

เมือง *[meu-ung]* country *(informal word)*

อังกฤษ *[ung-grìt]* England, Britain, English, British

ฝรั่ง *[fa-rùng]* European, Caucasian

ฝรั่งเศส *[fa-rùng-sàyt]* France, French

เยอรมัน *[yer-ra-mun]* Germany, German

ชาวเขา *[chao kǎo]* hill-tribe person/ people

แขก *[kàirk]* Indian, Malaysian

อินโดนีเซีย *[in-doh-nee-see-a]* Indonesia, Indonesian

ญี่ปุ่น *[yêe-bpÒOn]* Japan, Japanese

กะเหรี่ยง *[ga-rèe-ung]* Karen *(hill tribe)*

เขมร *[ka-mǎyn]* Cambodia (Kampuchea), Khmer, Cambodian

เกาหลี *[gao-lěe]* Korea, Korean

ภาษา *[pah-sǎh]* language

ลาว *[lao]* Laos, Lao

มาเลเซีย *[mah-lay-see-a]* Malaysia, Malaysian

แม้ว *[máy-o]* Meo, Hmong *(hill tribe)*

คน *[kon]* person, people

ชาว *[chao]* person, people

ฟิลิปปินส์ *[fin-lip-bpin]* Philippines, Filipino

รัสเซีย *[rút-see-a]* Russia, Russian

ซาอุ *[sah ÒO]* Saudi Arabia

สิงคโปร์ *[sǐng-ka-bpoh]* Singapore

ไทย *[tai]* Thai

สหรัฐอเมริกา *[sa-hà-rút a-may-ri-gah]* United States of America

ญวน *[yoo-un]* Vietnamese

เย้า *[yáo]* Yao *(hill tribe)*

CULTURAL INTEREST

เมืองโบราณ *[meu-ung boh-rahn]* Ancient City

กรมศิลปากร *[grom sĭn-la-bpah-gorn]* Department of Fine Arts

ตลาดน้ำ *[dta-làht náhm]* Floating Market

พิพิธภัณฑ์สถานแห่งชาติ *[pi-pít-ta-pun sa-tǎhn hàirng châht]* National Museum

โรงละครแห่งชาติ *[rohng la-korn hàirng châht]* National Theatre/Theater

พระบรมมหาราชวัง *[pra-ba-rom-ma-hǎh-râht-cha-wung]* Royal Palace

วัด *[wút]* temple

วัดพระแก้ว *[wút pra-kâir-o]* Temple of the Emerald Buddha

มวยไทย *[moo-ay tai]* Thai boxing

รำไทย *[rum tai]* Thai dancing

วัดโพธิ์ *[wút poh]* Wat Po

CUSTOMS

ศุลกากร *[sǒon-la-gah-gorn]* customs

มีของต้องสำแดง *[mee kǒrng dtôrng sǔm-dairng]* goods to declare

ตรวจคนเข้าเมือง *[dtròo-ut kon kâo meu-ung]* immigration

ไม่มีของต้องสำแดง *[mâi mee kǒrng dtôrng sǔm-dairng]* nothing to declare

เฉพาะหนังสือเดินทางไทย *[cha-pòr núng-sěu dern-tahng tai]* Thai passport holders only

DAYS

วันจันทร์ *[wun jun]* Monday

วันอังคาร *[wun ung-kahn]* Tuesday

วันพุธ *[wun póot]* Wednesday

วันพฤหัส *[wun pa-réu-hùt]* Thursday

วันศุกร์ *[wun sòok]* Friday

วันเสาร์ *[wun sǎo]* Saturday

วันอาทิตย์ *[wun ah-tít]* Sunday

วันพระ *[wun prá]* Buddhist holy day

วัน *[wun]* day

วันหยุด *[wun yòot]* holiday

วันขึ้นปีใหม่ *[wun kêun bpee mài]* New Year's Day

วันหยุดราชการ *[wun yòot râht-cha-gahn]* public holiday

วันสงกรานต์ *[wun sǒng-grahn]* Songkran Day *(Thai New Year)*

วันนี้ *[wun née]* today

พรุ่งนี้ *[prôong née]* tomorrow

วันเสาร์-อาทิตย์ *[wun sáo ah-tít]* weekend

เมื่อวานนี้ *[mêu-a wahn née]* yesterday

DEPARTMENT STORE SECTIONS

สุขภัณฑ์ *[sòok-ka-pun]* bathroom accessories

ที่จ่ายเงิน *[têe jài ngern]* cashier

แผนกเด็ก *[pa-nàirk dèk]* children's department

เครื่องสำอาง *[krêu-ung sǔm-ahng]* cosmetics

แผนกไฟฟ้า *[pa-nàirk fai fáh]* electrical goods

เครื่องเรือน *[krêu-ung reu-un]* furniture

วิทยุ-ทีวี *[wít-ta-yóO - tee-wee]* radio - TV

ห้องอาหาร *[hôrng ah-hǎhn]* restaurant

รองเท้า *[rorng-táo]* shoes

อุปกรณ์กีฬา *[òO-bpa-gorn gee-lah]* sports equipment

ของเล่นเด็ก *[kǒrng lên dèk]* toys

นาฬิกา *[nah-li-gah]* watches

DOCTORS *see* **MEDICAL**

DO NOT …

ห้าม *[hâhm …]* … forbidden, do not …

อย่า … *[yàh …]* do not …

โรงพยาบาล ห้ามใช้เสียง *[rohng pa-yah-bahn: hâhm chái sěe-ung]* hospital: no sounding horns

ห้ามผ่าน *[hâhm pàhn]* no admission

ห้ามเข้า *[hâhm kâo]* no entry

ผู้ไม่มีกิจห้ามเข้า *[pôo mâi mee gìt hâhm kâo]* no entry to unauthorized persons

ห้ามทิ้งขยะ *[hâhm tíng ka-yà]* no litter

ห้ามจอด *[hâhm jòrt]* no parking

ห้ามถ่ายรูป *[hâhm tài rôop]* no photographs

ห้ามสูบบุหรี่ *[hâhm sòop bOO-rèe]* no smoking

กรุณาอย่าส่งเสียงดัง *[ga-rOO-nah yàh sòng sěe-ung dung]* please don't make a noise

โปรดถอดรองเท้า *[bpròht tòrt rorng táo]* please remove your shoes

โปรดเงียบ *[bpròht ngêe-up]* silence, please

DRINKS

สุรา *[sǒo-rah]* alcoholic drink

เบียร์ *[bee-a]* beer

เบียร์อมฤต *[bee-a a-ma-rít]* Amarit beer *(tm)*

ขวด *[kòo-ut]* bottle

ขวดละ *[kòo-ut la ...]* ... per bottle

โคล่า *[koh-lâh]* Coca-Cola *(tm)*

น้ำมะพร้าว *[núm ma-práo]* coconut juice

กาแฟ *[gah-fair]* coffee

เครื่องดื่ม *[krêu-ung dèum]* drink

แฟนต้า *[fairn-dtâh]* Fanta *(tm)*

น้ำส้มคั้น *[núm sôm kún]* fresh orange juice

น้ำผลไม้ *[núm pǒn-la-mái]* fruit juice

แก้ว *[gâir-o]* glass

แก้วละ *[gâir-o la ...]* ... per glass

กรีนสปอต *[green-sa-bpòrt]* Green Spot *(tm)*, fizzy orange

กาแฟเย็น *[gah-fair yen]* iced coffee

เบียร์คลอสเตอร์ *[bee-a klòrt-sa-dter]* Kloster beer *(tm)*

น้ำมะนาว *[núm ma-nao]* lime

นมสด *[nom sòt]* milk

แม่โขง *[mâir kǒhng]* Mekhong Whisky *(tm)*

น้ำส้ม *[núm sôm]* orange

เป๊ปซี่ *[bpép-sêe]* Pepsi-Cola *(tm)*

น้ำโปลาริส *[náhm bpoh-lah-rít]* Polaris water *(tm)*, bottled drinking water from artesian well

เซเวนอัพ *[say-wen úp]* Seven-Up *(tm)*

เบียร์สิงห์ *[bee-a sǐng]* Singha beer *(tm)*

สไปรท์ *[sa-bprai]* Sprite *(tm)*

น้ำโซดา *[núm soh-dah]* soda water

น้ำชา *[núm chah]* tea

กวางทอง *[gwahng torng]* Kwang Torng Whisky *(tm)*

โอเลี้ยง *[oh-lée-ung]* very sweet ice

black coffee

น้ำ *[náhm]* water

ELEVATORS *see* LIFTS

EMERGENCIES

โรงพยาบาล *[rohng pa-yah-bahn]* hospital

ตำรวจ *[dtum-ròo-ut]* police

FOOD

Starters

ขนมจีบ *[ka-nǒm jèep]* 'dim-sum' small balls of minced/ground pork wrapped in pastry and steamed

ปอเปี๊ยะ *[bpor bpêe-a]* Thai spring roll

หมูสะเต๊ะ *[mǒo sa-dtáy]* pork satay, thin strips of charcoal-grilled pork

ทอดมัน *[tôrt mun]* 'tort mun', finely minced/ground shrimps or fish, fried in batter with spices

Soups and curries

แกงเนื้อ *[gairng néu-a]* beef curry

แกงส้ม *[gairng sôm]* bitter flavo(u)red curry

แกงจืด *[gairng jèut]* bland vegetable soup or stock eaten with spicier curry dishes

ไก่ต้มข่า *[gài dtôm kàh]* chicken boiled in spicy stock

แกงไก่ *[gairng gài]* chicken curry

ต้มยำไก่ *[dtôm yum gài]* chicken 'tom yam', a spicy soup dish

พะแนง *[pa-nairng]* dry curry

ต้มยำปลา *[dtôm yum bplah]* fish 'tom yam', a spicy soup dish

แกงกาหรี่ *[gairng gah-rèe]* Indian curry

แกงมัสหมั่น *[gairng mút-sa-mùn]* Muslim curry

ต้มยำกุ้ง *[dtôm yum gÔOng]* shrimp 'tom yam', a spicy soup dish

แกงเผ็ด *[gairng pèt]* spicy curry

แกง *[gairng]* wet curry

Egg dishes

ไข่ *[kài]* egg

ไข่พะโล้ *[kài pa-lóh]* egg stewed in soy sauce

ไข่เจียว *[kài jee-o]* flat, deep-fried 'omelet(te)'

ไข่ดาว *[kài dao]* fried egg

ไข่ยัดไส้ *[kài yút sâi]* stuffed omelet(te)

ไข่ลูกเขย *[kài lôok kěr-ee]* 'son-in-law eggs', hard-boiled egg garnished with various condiments

ไข่ลวก *[kài lôo-uk]* very soft boiled egg, eaten almost raw

Fish and fish dishes

ปู *[bpoo]* crab

ปลา *[bplah]* fish

กุ้ง *[gÔOng]* shrimp

กุ้งผัดใบกระเพรา *[gÔOng pùt bai gra-prao]* shrimps fried with basil leaves

กุ้งผัดพริก *[gÔOng pùt prík]* shrimps fried with chillies

ปลาหมึก *[bplah-mèuk]* squid

ปลาผัดเปรี้ยวหวาน *[bplah pùt bprêe-o wǎhn]* sweet and sour fish

Meat and meat dishes

เนื้อ *[néu-a]* beef

เนื้อผัดน้ำมันหอย *[néu-a pùt núm mun hǒy]* beef fried in oyster sauce

เนื้อผัดพริก *[néu-a pùt prík]* beef fried with chillies

เนื้อผัดขิง *[néu-a pùt kǐng]* beef fried with ginger

ไก่ *[gài]* chicken

ไก่ผัดหน่อไม้ *[gài pùt nòr mái]* chicken fried with bamboo shoots

ไก่ผัดใบกระเพรา *[gài pùt bai gra-prao]* chicken fried with basil leaves

ไก่ผัดพริก *[gài pùt prík]* chicken fried with chillies

ไก่ทอดกระเทียมพริกไทย *[gài tôrt gra-tee-um prík tai]* chicken fried with garlic and pepper

ไก่ผัดขิง *[gài pùt kǐng]* chicken fried with ginger

เป็ด *[bpèt]* duck

หมู *[mǒo]* pork

หมูผัดหน่อไม้ *[mǒo pùt nòr mái]* pork fried with bamboo shoots

หมูผัดใบกระเพรา *[mǒo pùt bai gra-prao]* pork fried with basil leaves

หมูผัดพริก *[mǒo pùt prík]* pork fried with chillies

หมูทอดกระเทียมพริกไทย *[mǒo tôrt gra-tee-um prík tai]* pork fried with garlic and pepper

หมูผัดขิง *[mǒo pùt kǐng]* pork fried with ginger

หมูพะโล้ *[mǒo pa-lóh]* pork stewed in soy sauce

ไก่ย่าง *[gài yâhng]* roast/barbecued chicken

ไก่ผัดเปรี้ยวหวาน *[gài pùt bprêe-o wǎhn]* sweet and sour chicken

หมูผัดเปรี้ยวหวาน *[mǒo pùt bprêe-o wǎhn]* sweet and sour pork

Salads

ส้มตำ *[sôm dtum]* salad made of sliced green papaya, tomato, chillies, dried shrimps or crab and flavo(u)red with sugar, shrimp sauce and peanuts

ยำ *[yum]* Thai salad

Rice and rice dishes

ข้าว (สวย) *[kâo (sǒo-ay)]* boiled rice

ข้าวผัดไก่ *[kâo pùt gài]* chicken fried rice

ข้าวมันไก่ *[kâo mun gài]* chicken rice

ข้าวผัดปู *[kâo pùt bpoo]* crab fried rice

ข้าวแกง *[kâo gairng]* curry and rice

ข้าวหน้าเป็ด *[kâo nâh bpèt]* duck rice

ข้าวผัด *[kâo pùt]* fried rice

ข้าวผัดหมู *[kâo pùt mŏo]* pork fried rice

ข้าวหมูแดง *[kâo mŏo dairng]* red pork rice

ข้าวคลุกกะปิ *[kâo klóok ga-bpì]* rice fried with shrimp paste and served with sweet pork and shredded omelet(te)

ข้าวต้ม *[kâo dtôm]* rice gruel, 'rice porridge'

ข้าวผัดกุ้ง *[kâo pùt gÔong]* shrimp fried rice

ข้าวเหนียว *[kâo nĕe-o]* sticky rice

Noodles and noodle dishes

บะหมี่แห้ง *[ba-mèe hâirng]* 'dry' egg noodles *(i.e. without the soup)*

ก๋วยเตี๋ยวแห้ง *[gŏo-ay dtĕe-o hâirng]* 'dry' noodles *(i.e. without the soup)*

ผัดซีอิ๊ว *[pùt see éw]* Chinese-style fried noodles in soy sauce

หมี่กรอบ *[mèe gròrp]* crispy noodles

บะหมี่น้ำ *[ba-mèe náhm]* egg noodle soup

บะหมี่ *[ba-mèe]* egg noodles

เส้นใหญ่-เส้นเล็ก-เส้นหมี่ *[sên yài - sên lék - sên mèe]* large - small - very small *(referring to the width of noodles)*

ก๋วยเตี๋ยวน้ำ *[gŏo-ay dtĕe-o náhm]* noodle soup

ก๋วยเตี๋ยว *[gŏo-ay dtĕe-o]* noodles made from rice flour

ผัดลาดหน้า *[pùt lâht nâh]* noodles with fried vegetables and meat in a thick gravy

ขนมจีน *[ka-nŏm jeen]* Thai vermicelli

ผัดไทย *[pùt tai]* Thai-style fried noodles

วุ้นเส้น *[wÓon-sên]* transparent noodles

Vegetables and vegetable dishes

หน่อไม้ *[nòr mái]* bamboo shoots

ถั่วงอก *[tòo-a ngôrk]* beansprouts

พริก *[prík]* chilli

แตงกวา *[dtairng gwah]* cucumber

ผัดผักบุ้งไฟแดง *[pùt pùk bÔong fai dairng]* fried 'Morning Glory'

กระเทียม *[gra-tee-um]* garlic

ขิง *[kĭng]* ginger

พริกหยวก *[prík yòo-uk]* green pepper

ผักบุ้ง *[pùk bÔong]* 'Morning Glory', a common vegetable with pointed leaves similar to bindweed; it is usually fried and served with a gravy

เห็ด *[hèt]* mushrooms

หัวหอม *[hŏo-a hŏrm]* onions

ถั่วลันเตา *[tòo-a lun-dtao]* small sweet peas *(eaten together with the pod)*

ผักคะน้า *[pùk ka-náh]* spring greens

ต้นหอม *[dtôn hŏrm]* spring onions

ข้าวโพด *[kâo pôht]* sweet corn

มะเขือเทศ *[ma-kĕu-a-tâyt]* tomatoes

ผัก *[pùk]* vegetables

Fruit

กล้วย *[glôo-ay]* banana

มะพร้าว *[ma-práo]* coconut

น้อยหน่า *[nóy-nàh]* custard apple, about the size of an orange; the coarse green skin falls away easily when ripe; inside, very sweet white flesh surrounds numerous individual black seeds

ทุเรียน *[dtOO-ree-un]* durian, a large fruit often considerably larger than a rugby ball or an American football; on the outside it has a thick green prickly skin, while inside the fruit is yellow and soft in texture; famed for its pungent smell

ผลไม้ *[pŏn-la-mái]* fruit

ฝรั่ง *[fa-rùng]* guava, approximately the size of a lemon with a green skin - which is eaten - and white flesh; the core of the fruit contains numerous tiny brown seeds

ขนุน *[ka-nŎon]* jackfruit, a large fruit about the size of a rugby ball or an American football with a coarse green skin; inside the fruit is yellow, and has a sweet flavo(u)r and a leathery texture

ลำใย *[lum-yai]* longan, a small spherical fruit somewhat resembling an oak-apple in size and colo(u)r; underneath the brittle skin, white flesh surrounds ạ blackish stone

ลิ้นจี่ *[lín-jèe]* lychee

มะม่วง *[ma-môo-ung]* mango

มังคุด *[mung-kóOt]* mangosteen, a small spherical fruit, approximately the size of a mandarin orange; the skin is purple and very thick, while the flesh inside is white and formed into distinct segments

ส้ม *[sôm]* orange

มะละกอ *[ma-la-gor]* papaya, an oblong-shaped fruit about a foot long with an outer skin that varies in colo(u)r from green to yellow; inside the flesh, when ripe, is reddish orange, soft in texture and has numerous tiny black pips

สับปะรด *[sùp-bpa-rót]* pineapple

ส้มโอ *[sôm oh]* pomelo, very similar to a grapefruit, but rather larger with a thick green outer skin

เงาะ *[ngór]* rambutan, a small fruit about the size of a plum, with a coarse red or sometimes yellowish skin which is covered in soft prickles; the white flesh inside surrounds a large stone, and, when ripe, is very sweet

ชมพู่ *[chom-pôo]* rose apple, similar in shape to a strawberry but somewhere between a strawberry and apple in size; the skin, which is eaten, can be either red, pink or green, while the flesh inside has a woolly texture

ละมุด *[la-móOt]* sapodilla, a small brown fruit, approximately the size of plum, with a texture somewhat similar to a pear

แตงโม *[dtairng-moh]* water melon

Sweets

ไอศครีม *['ice cream']* ice cream

ข้าวเหนียวมะม่วง *[kâo něe-o ma-môo-ung]* mango with sticky rice

Basics

น้ำพริก *[núm prík]* chilli paste

น้ำปลา *[núm bplah]* fish sauce

พริกไทย *[prík tai]* pepper

น้ำซีอิ๊ว *[núm see éw]* soy sauce

น้ำส้ม *[núm sôm]* vinegar

Methods of preparation/cooking

ย่าง *[yâhng]* barbecued, charcoal-grilled

ต้ม *[dtôm]* boiled

ทอด *[tôrt]* deep-fried

อบ *[òp]* over-cooked

ผัด *[pùt]* stir-fried

ปิ้ง *[bpîng]* toasted

Menu terms & notices

เครื่องดื่ม *[krêu-ung dèum]* drinks

รายการอาหาร *[rai gahn ah-hǎhn]* menu

ราคา *[rah-kah]* price

FORMS

ที่อยู่ *[têe yòo]* address

อายุ *[ah-yóO]* age

พ.ศ. *[por sǒr]* (year)... B.E. *(543 years later than A.D.)*

สีตา *[sěe dtah]* colo(u)r of eyes

สีผม *[sěe pǒm]* colo(u)r of hair

เกิดวันที่ *[gèrt wun-têe]* date of birth

อำเภอ *[um-per]* Amphoe, district

ตั้งแต่ ... ถึง *[dtûng-dtàir ... těung ...]* from ... until ...

ความสูง *[kwahm sǒong]* height

บ้านเลขที่ *[bâhn lâyk têe]* house number

ตรอก *[dtròrk]* lane

บันทึก *[bun-téuk]* memo

เดือน *[deu-un]* month

ชื่อ *[chêu]* (Christian) name

สัญชาติ *[sǔn-châht]* nationality

หมายเหตุ *[măi-hàyt]* note *(n.b.)*
อาชีพ *[ah-chêep]* occupation
หนังสือเดินทางหมายเลข *[núng-sĕu dern tahng măi-lâyk]* passport number
จังหวัด *[jung-wùt]* Province
เชื้อชาติ *[chéu-a châht]* race
อยู่ที่ *[yòo têe]* residing at
ถนน *[ta-nŏn]* road
เพศ *[pâyt]* sex
ลายเซ็น *[lai sen]* signature
ลงชื่อ *[long chêu]* signed
ซอย *[soy]* soy, lane
พักที่ *[púk têe]* staying at
ตำบล *[dtum-bon]* Tambon, sub-district
นามสกุล *[nahm sa-gOOn]* surname
หมู่บ้าน *[mòo-bâhn]* village
น้ำหนัก *[núm nùk]* weight
พยาน *[pa-yahn]* witness

GARAGES

บริการซ่อมรถ *[bor-ri-gahn sôrm rót]* car repair service
บริการล้างรถ *[bor-ri-gahn láhng rót]* car wash service
เปลี่ยนหม้อกรอง *[bplèe-un môr grorng]* filters changed
อู่ *[òo]* garage
บริการ 24 ช.ม. *[bor-ri-gahn yêe-sìp-sèe chôo-a-mohng]* 24-hour service
ห้ามสูบบุหรี่ *[hâhm sòop bOO-rèe]* no smoking
เปลี่ยนน้ำมันเครื่อง *[bplèe-un núm mun krêu-ung]* oil changed
บริการอัดฉีด *[bor-ri-gahn ùt chèet]* pressurized air
ปะยาง *[bpà yahng]* punctures repaired
เครื่องอะไหล่ *[krêu-ung a-lài]* spare parts

GEOGRAPHICAL

แม่น้ำเจ้าพระยา *[mâir-náhm jâo pra-yah]*
Chao Phraya River
ชายแดน *[chai dairn]* border
เขต *[kàyt]* boundary, area
คลอง *[klorng]* canal
เมืองหลวง *[meu-ung lŏo-ung]* capital city
ภาคกลาง *[pâhk glahng]* central region
ประเทศ *[bpra-tâyt]* country
ชนบท *[chon-na-bòt]* countryside
อำเภอ *[um-per]* Amphoe, district
ป่าดงดิบ *[bpàh dong dìp]* forest, jungle
เขา *[kăo]* hill
เกาะ *[gòr]* island
ป่า *[bpàh]* jungle, forest
แม่โขง *[mâir-kŏhng]* Mekhong River
ภาคอีสาน *[pâhk ee-săhn]* north-eastern region
ภาคเหนือ *[pâhk nĕu-a]* northern region
ที่ราบลุ่ม *[têe râhp lOOm]* plain
จังหวัด *[jung-wùt]* province
แม่น้ำ *[mâir-náhm]* river
ทะเล *[ta-lay]* sea
ชายทะเล *[chai ta-lay]* seaside
ภาคใต้ *[pâhk dtâi]* southern region
ตำบล *[dtum-bon]* Tambon, sub-district
เมือง *[meu-ung]* town, city, country
ต่างจังหวัด *[dtàhng jung-wùt]* up-country
บ้านนอก *[bâhn-nôrk]* up-country
หมู่บ้าน *[mòo-bâhn]* village

GREETINGS

bpai năi?
literally: where are you going? - used as a general greeting - reply: bpai têe-o *(literally: just round and about)*

bpai năi mah?
literally: where have you been? - used as a general greeting - reply: bpai têe-o mah *(literally: I've been just round and about)*

bpen yung-ngai bâhng?
how are you? - reply: sa-bai dee krúp (kâ)

sa-bai dee lěr krúp (kâ)
are you well? - reply: sa-bai dee krúp (kâ)

sa-wùt dee krúp (kâ)
hello, good morning, good afternoon, good evening *(a more formal greeting)* - reply: sa-wùt dee krúp (kâ)

HAIRDRESSER

เสริมสวย *[sěrm sǒo-ay]* beauty care

นวดหน้า *[nôo-ut nâh]* facial massage

ตัดผม *[dtùt pǒm]* hair cut

เป่าผม *[bpào pǒm]* hair drying

ไดผม *[dai pǒm]* hair drying

สระผม *[sà pǒm]* hair wash

ตัดเล็บ *[dtùt lép]* manicure

ดัดผม *[dùt pǒm]* perm

เซทผม *[sét pǒm]* set

โกนหนวด *[gohn nòo-ut]* shave

HISTORICAL INTEREST

เมืองโบราณ *[meu-ung boh-rahn]* Ancient City

อยุธยา *[a-yóo-ta-yah]* Ayuthaya

บางปะอิน *[bahng bpà-in]* Bang Pa-In

เชียงใหม่ *[chee-ung mài]* Chiangmai

พิพิธภัณฑ์ *[pi-pít-ta-pun]* museum

นครปฐม *[na-korn bpa-tǒm]* Nakorn Pathom

พิมาย *[pi-mai]* Phimai

พระปฐมเจดีย์ *[prá-bpa-tǒm jay-dee]* Pra Pathom Jedi

แม่น้ำแคว *[mâir-náhm kwair]* River Kwai

พระบรมมหาราชวัง *[prá-ba-rom-ma-hǎh-râtch-a-wung]* The Royal Palace

วังสวนผักกาด *[wúng sǒo-un pùk-gàht]* Suan Pakkard Palace

สุโขทัย *[sòo-kǒh-tai]* Sukhothai

วัด *[wút]* temple

วัดพระแก้ว *[wút pra-kâir-o]* Temple of the Emerald Buddha

วัดโพธิ์ *[wút poh]* Wat Po

HOSPITALS *see* MEDICAL

HOTELS

คอฟฟี่ช้อป *[kórp-fee chórp]* coffee shop

ห้องคู่ *[hôrng kôo]* double room

ห้องคู่ปรับอากาศ *[hôrng kôo bprùp ah-gàht]* double room with air-conditioning

ชั้น *[chún]* floor

สอบถาม *[sòrp tǎhm]* inquiries

ห้องน้ำสตรี *[hôrng náhm sa-dtree]* ladies' toilet/rest room

ลิฟท์ *[lif]* lift, elevator

บริการรถรับส่ง *[bor-ri-gahn rót rúp sòng]* limousine service

ห้องน้ำบุรุษ *[hôrng náhm bOO-ròOt]* men's toilet/rest room

ห้ามสูบบุหรี่ *[hâhm sòop bOO-rèe]* no smoking

แผนกต้อนรับ *[pa-nàirk dtôrn rúp]* reception

ห้องอาหาร *[hôrng ah-hǎhn]* restaurant

ห้อง *[hôrng]* room

บริการนำเที่ยว *[bor-ri-gahn num têe-o]* sight-seeing tours

ห้องเดี่ยว *[hôrng dèe-o]* single room

ห้องเดี่ยวปรับอากาศ *[hôrng dèe-o bprùp ah-gàht]* single room with air-conditioning

สระว่ายน้ำ *[sà wâi náhm]* swimming pool

ยินดีต้อนรับ *[yin dee dtôrn rúp]* welcome

LIFTS

ลง *[long]* down

ชั้น *[chún]* floor

ลิฟท์ *[lif]* lift, elevator

ไม่เกิน ... คน *[mâi gern ... kon]* maximum load ... people

ห้ามสูบบุหรี่ *[hâhm sòop bOO-rèe]* no smoking

ขึ้น *[kêun]* up

MEDICAL

รถพยาบาล *[rót pa-yah-bahn]* ambulance

คุมกำเนิด *[kOOm gum-nèrt]* birth control

ตรวจเลือด *[dtròo-ut lêu-ut]* blood test

ห้างขายยา *[hâhng kǎi yah]* chemist, drug store

คลีนิค *[klee-ník]* clinic

ห้องคลอด *[hôrng klôrt]* delivery room

ทำฟัน *[tum fun]* dental surgery, dentist

ทันตแพทย์ *[tun-dta-pâirt]* dentist

จำหน่ายยา *[jum-nài yah]* dispensary

แพทย์หญิง *[pâirt yǐng]* doctor *(female)*

พ.ญ. *[pâirt yǐng]* (abbreviation) doctor *(female)*

นายแพทย์ *[nai pâirt]* doctor *(male)*

น.พ. *[nai pâirt]* (abbreviation) doctor *(male)*

ตรวจสายตา *[dtròo-ut sǎi-dtah]* eye-testing

โรงพยาบาล *[rohng pa-yah-bahn]* hospital

ฉีดยา *[chèet yah]* injections

นางพยาบาล *[nahng pa-yah-bahn]* nurse

ตรวจปัสสาวะ *[dtròo-ut bpùt-sǎh-wá]* urine test

เอ็กซเรย์ *['X-ray']* X-ray

MEDICINE LABELS

หลังอาหาร *[lǔng ah-hǎhn]* after meals

ทา *[tah]* apply *(ointments)*

ก่อนนอน *[gòrn norn]* before going to bed

ก่อนอาหาร *[gòrn ah-hǎhn]* before meals

ยาอันตราย *[yah un-dta-rai]* dangerous medicine

วิธีใช้ *[wí-tee chái]* instructions for use

ยา *[yah]* medicine

เม็ด *[mét]* tablet, pill

วันละ ... เม็ด *[wun la ... mét]* ... tablets per day

รับประทาน *[rúp-bpra-tahn]* take *(orally)*

ช้อนชา *[chórn chah]* teaspoon

วันละ ... ครั้ง *[wun la ... krúng]* ... times per day

MONTHS

มกราคม *[mók-ga-rah-kom]* January

กุมภาพันธ์ *[gOOm-pah-pun]* February

มีนาคม *[mee-nah-kom]* March

เมษายน *[may-sǎh-yon]* April

พฤษภาคม *[préut-sa-pah-kom]* May

มิถุนายน *[mí-tOO-nah-yon]* June

กรกฎาคม *[ga-rúk-ga-dah-kom]* July

สิงหาคม *[sǐng-hǎh-kom]* August

กันยายน *[gun-yah-yon]* September

ตุลาคม *[dtOO-lah-kom]* October

พฤศจิกายน *[préut-sa-jìk-gah-yon]* November

ธันวาคม *[tun-wah-kom]* December

ต้นเดือน *[dtôn deu-un]* beginning of the month

เดือนก่อน *[deu-un gòrn]* last month

กลางเดือน *[glahng deu-un]* mid-month

เดือน *[deu-un]* month

เดือนหน้า *[deu-un nâh]* next month

ปลายเดือน *[bplai deu-un]* the end of the month

เดือนนี้ *[deu-un née]* this month

MOVIE THEATERS *see* **CINEMAS**

NIGHT SPOTS

บาร์ *[bah]* bar

โบลลิ่ง *[bohn-lîng]* bowling

โรงภาพยนตร์ *[rohng pâhp-pá-yon]* cinema, movie theater

คอฟฟี่ ช็อบ *[kórp-fee chórp]* coffee shop

ดิสโก้ *[dít-sa-gôh]* disco

อาบ อบ นวด *[àhp òb nôo-ut]* massage

ไนท์คลับ *[nái klùp]* night club

สวนอาหาร *[sǒo-un ah-hǎhn]* open-air restaurant

ห้องอาหาร *[hôrng ah-hǎhn]* restaurant

ภัตตาคาร *[pút-dtah-kahn]* restaurant

ร้านอาหาร *[ráhn ah-hǎhn]* restaurant

NOTICES IN SHOPS

ใบละ ... บาท *[bai la ... bàht]* ... baht each (e.g. for eggs, fruit)

ลูกละ ... บาท *[lôok la ... bàht]* ... baht each (e.g. for large fruit)

ตัวละ ... บาท *[dtoo-a la ... bàht]* ... baht each (e.g. items of clothing)

โลละ ... บาท *[loh la ... bàht]* ... baht per kilo

ชิ้นละ ... บาท *[chín la ... bàht]* ... baht per piece/portion

บาท *[bàht]* baht (unit of currency)

คู่ละ ... บาท *[kôo la ... bàht]* baht per pair (e.g. shoes)

ที่จ่ายเงิน *[têe jài ngern]* cash desk

ราคา *[rah-kah]* price

ลดราคา *[lót rah-kah]* sale

ลดพิเศษ *[lót pi-sàyt]* special reductions

NOTICES ON DOORS

เฉพาะเจ้าหน้าที่ *[cha-pór jâo-nâh-têe]* authorized personnel only

กริ่ง *[grìng]* bell

ระวังสุนัขดุ *[ra-wung sOO-núk dÒO]* beware of the dog

หมาดุ *[mǎh dÒO]* beware of the dog

เข้า *[kâo]* in

ห้ามเข้า *[hâhm kâo]* no entry

ไม่มีกิจห้ามเข้า *[mâi mee gìt hâhm kâo]* no entry to unauthorized persons

ห้ามจอด *[hâhm jòrt]* no parking

ห้ามจอดรถขวางประตู *[hâhm jòrt rót kwǎhng bpra-dtoo]* no parking in front of the gate

ห้ามกลับรถ *[hâhm glùp rót]* no turning

ออก *[òrk]* out

กรุณาถอดรองเท้า *[ga-rOO-nah tòrt rorng táo]* please remove your shoes

กรุณากดกริ่ง *[ga-rOO-nah gòt grìng]* please ring

กด *[gòt]* press

ถนนส่วนบุคคล *[ta-nǒn sòo-un bÒOk-kon]* private road

ดึง *[deung]* pull

ผลัก *[plùk]* push

ทางเข้า *[tahng kâo]* way in

ทางออก *[tahng òrk]* way out

PLACE NAMES

อยุธยา *[a-yÓOt-ta-yah]* Ayutthaya

บางปะอิน *[bahng-bpà-in]* Bang Pa-In

กรุงเทพฯ *[grOOng-tâyp]* Bangkok

บางลำภู *[bahng-lum-poo]* Banglamphu

เชียงใหม่ *[chêe-ung-mài]* Chiangmai

อนุสาวรีย์ประชาธิปไตย *[a-nÓO-sǎh-wa-ree bpra-chah-típ-bpa-dtai]* Democracy Monument

หาดใหญ่ *[hàht yài]* Hat Yai

หัวหิน *[hǒo-a hin]* Hua Hin

หัวลำโพง *[hǒo-a lum-pohng]* Hua Lampong

กาญจนบุรี *[gahn-ja-na-bOO-ree]* Kanchanaburi

ขอนแก่น *[kǒrn-gàirn]* Khonkaen

เกาะสมุย *[gòr sa-mǒo-ee]* Koh Samui

สวนลุมพินี *[sǒo-un lOOm-pi-nee]* Lumpini Park

นครปฐม *[na-korn bpà-tom]* Nakhorn Pathom

นครราชสีมา *[na-korn râht-cha-si-mah]* Nakhorn Ratchasima

พัทยา *[pút-ta-yah]* Pattaya

ภูเก็ต *[poo-gèt]* Phuket

ประตูน้ำ *[bpra-dtOO náhm]* Pratu Nam

สนามหลวง *[sa-nǎhm lǒo-ung]* Sanam Luang

สยามแสควร์ *[sa-yǎhm sa-kwair]* Siam Square

สงขลา *[sǒng-klǎh]* Songkhla

สุโขทัย *[sÒo-kǒh-tai]* Sukhothai

ธนบุรี *[ton-bOO-ree]* Thonburi

อุบลราชธานี *[OO-bon râht-cha-tah-nee]* Ubonratchathani

อนุสาวรีย์ชัยสมรภูมิ *[a-nOO-sǎh-wa-ree chai sa-mǒr-ra-poom]* Victory Monument

เยาวราช *[yao-wa-râht]* Yaowarat *(China Town area of Bangkok)*

POST OFFICES

กรุงเทพฯ *[grOOng-tâyp]* Bangkok

ตู้จดหมาย *[dtôo jòt-mǎi]* letter box

ที่อื่น *[têe èun]* other places

พัสดุ *[pút-sa-dÒO]* parcels

ที่ทำการไปรษณีย์ *[têe tum gahn bprai-sa-nee]* post office

ลงทะเบียน *[long ta-bee-un]* registered mail

ไปรษณียากร *[bprai-sa-nee-yah-gorn]* stamps

โทรเลข *[toh-ra-lâyk]* telegrams

โทรศัพท์ *[toh-ra-sùp]* telephone

PUBLIC BUILDINGS

สนามบิน *[sa-nǎhm bin]* airport

ธนาคาร *[ta-nah-kahn]* bank

สนามมวย *[sa-nǎhm moo-ay]* boxing stadium

สถานีรถเมล์ *[sa-tǎhn-nee rót may]* bus station

โรงภาพยนตร์ *[rohng pâhp-pa-yon]* cinema, movie theater

คลีนิค *[klee-ník]* clinic

วิทยาลัย *[wít-ta-yah-lai]* college

กรมศุลกากร *[grom sǒOn-la-gah-gorn]* Customs Department

กรม *[grom]* department *(of government)*

ที่ว่าการอำเภอ *[têe wâh gahn um-per]* district office

กอง *[gorng]* division *(of government)*

สถานทูต *[sa-tǎhn tôot]* embassy

สนามกอล์ฟ *[sa-nǎhm górp]* golf course

โรงพยาบาล *[rohng pa-yah-bahn]* hospital

โรงแรม *[rohng rairm]* hotel

กองตรวจคนเข้าเมือง *[gorng dtròo-ut kon kâo meu-ung]* Immigration Division

กรมแรงงาน *[grom rairng ngahn]* Labour/Labor Department

ศาล *[sǎhn]* law court

ห้องสมุด *[hôrng sa-mÒOt]* library

ตลาด *[dta-làht]* market

กระทรวง *[gra-soo-ung]* ministry

พิพิธภัณฑ์ *[pí-pít-ta-pun]* museum

สนามกีฬาแห่งชาติ *[sa-nǎhm gee-lah hàirng châht]* National Stadium

สถานีตำรวจ *[sa-tǎhn-nee dtum-ròo-ut]* police station

ไปรษณีย์ *[bprai-sa-nee]* post office

โรงเรียน *[rohng ree-un]* school

ร้าน *[ráhn]* shop, store

ศูนย์การค้า *[sǒon gahn káh]* shopping centre/center

ห้าง *[hâhng]* store, shop

กรมสรรพากร *[grom sǔn-pah-gorn]* Tax Department

วัด *[wút]* temple

โรงละคร *[rohng la-korn]* theatre, theater

องค์การส่งเสริมการท่องเที่ยวแห่งประเทศไทย *[ong-gahn sòng sěrm gahn tôrng têe-o hàirng bpra-tâyt tai]* Tourist Organization of Thailand

สถานีรถไฟ *[sa-tǎhn-nee rót fai]* train station, railway station

มหาวิทยาลัย *[ma-hǎh-wít-ta-yah-lai]* university

RENTALS

อพาทเมนท์ให้เช่า *[ah-paht-mén hâi châo]* apartment for rent

ชั่วโมงละ ... บาท *[chôo-a mohng la ... bàht]* ... baht per hour

เดือนละ ... บาท *[deu-un la ... bàht]* ... baht per month

บาท *[bàht]* baht *(unit of currency)*

รถให้เช่า *[rót hâi châo]* car for hire/to rent

แฟลตให้เช่า *[flàirt hâi châo]* flat to let, apartment for rent

ให้เช่า *[hâi châo]* for hire, to let, to rent

บ้านให้เช่า *[bâhn hâi châo]* house to let/for rent

ค่าเช่า *[kâh châo]* rental, fee

ห้องให้เช่า *[hôrng hâi châo]* room to let/for rent

REPLIES

a-rai ná krúp (kâ)
pardon (me)?

kòrp-kOOn krúp (kâ)
thank you - reply: mâi bpen rai (you're welcome)

mâi kâo jai
I don't understand

pôot èek tee see krúp (kâ)
say it again please

RESTAURANTS AND BARS

บริการ 24 ช.ม. *[bor-ri-gahn 24 chôo-a mohng]* 24-hour service

ห้องแอร์ *[hôrng-air]* air-conditioned room

ร้านอาหารโต้รุ่ง *[ráhn ah-hǎhn dtôh rôOng]* all-night restaurant

บาร์ *[bah]* bar

ชาม *[chahm]* bowl, dish

อาหารจีน *[ah-hǎhn jeen]* Chinese food

คอฟฟี่ ช็อป *[kórp-fêe chórp]* coffee shop

อาหาร *[ah-hǎhn]* food

อาหารญี่ปุ่น *[ah-hǎhn yêe-bpOOn]* Japanese food

อาหารมุสลิม *[ah-hǎhn mOO-sa-lim]* Muslim food

อาหารอีสาน *[ah-hǎhn ee-sǎhn]* North-Eastern food

สวนอาหาร *[sǒo-un ah-hǎhn]* open-air restaurant

ชามละ *[chahm la ...]* ... per bowl/dish

จานละ *[jahn la ...]* per ... plate/dish

จาน *[jahn]* plate, dish

ราคา *[rah-kan]* price

เชลล์ชวนชิม *[chen choo-un chim Shell]* recommended *(tm)*, seal of approval, equivalent to Good Food Guide

ร้านอาหาร *[ráhn ah-hǎhn]* restaurant

ห้องอาหาร *[hông ah-hǎhn]* restaurant

ภัตตาคาร *[pút-dtah-kahn]* restaurant

อาหารทะเล *[ah-hǎhn ta-lay]* seafood

อาหารปักษ์ใต้ *[ah-hǎhn bpùk dtâi]* Southern food

อาหารไทย *[ah-hǎhn tai]* Thai food

อาหารฝรั่ง *[ah-hǎhn fa-rùng]* Western food

REST ROOMS *see* TOILETS

ROAD SIGNS

ทางโค้ง *[tahng kóhng]* bend

ระวัง *[ra-wung]* caution

ระวัง ทางขวางหน้าเป็นทางเอก *[ra-wung tahng kwǎhng nâh bpen tahng àyk]* caution: major road ahead

อันตราย *[un-dta-rai]* danger

ทางเบี่ยง *[tahng bèe-ung]* diversion

ขับช้า ๆ *[kùp cháh cháh]* drive slowly

หยุด-ตรวจ *[yòot-dtròo-ut]* halt - checkpoint

โรงพยาบาล ห้ามใช้เสียง *[rohng pa-yah-bahn hâhm chái sěe-ung]* hospital: no sounding horns

ชิดซ้าย *[chít sái]* keep left

40 ก.ม. *[sèe sìp gi-loh-mét]* 40 kilometres/kilometers

3 ม. *[sahm mét]* 3 metres/meters

ห้ามเข้า *[hâhm kâo]* no entry

ห้ามแซง *[hâhm sairng]* no overtaking, no passing

ห้ามจอด *[hâhm jòrt]* no parking

ห้ามรถทุกชนิด *[hâhm rót tóok cha-nít]* no vehicles

ทางรถไฟ *[tahng rót fai]* railway, railroad

หยุด *[yòot]* stop

โรงเรียน *[rohng ree-un]* school

4 ตัน *[sèe dtun]* 4 tons

ห้ามเลี้ยว *[hâhm lée-o]* no turning

ห้ามกลับรถ *[hâhm glùp rót]* no U-turns

SCHEDULES *see* **TIMETABLES**

STATIONS

จองตั๋วล่วงหน้า *[jorng dtǒo-a lôo-ung nâh]* advance bookings

ถึง *[těung]* arrives

ออก *[òrk]* departs

แผนกสอบถาม *[pa-nàirk sòrp tǎhm]* enquiries

รับฝากของ *[rúp fàhk kǒrng]* left luggage, baggage checkroom

ชานชาลา *[chahn-chah-lah]* platform, track

ประชาสัมพันธ์ *[bpra-chah sǔm-pun]* public relations

สถานีรถไฟ *[sa-tǎh-nee rót fai]* railway station, train station

ร.ฟ.ท. *[rót fai tai]* Thai State Railway/Railroad Authority

ที่จำหน่ายตั๋ว *[têe jum-nài dtǒo-a]* ticket office

กำหนดเวลาเดินรถ *[gum-nòt way-lah dern rót]* timetable, schedule

สุขา หญิง-ชาย *[sòo-kǎh yǐng - chai]* toilet/rest room ladies - men

รถไฟ *[rót fai]* train

ห้องพักผู้โดยสาร *[hôrng púk pôo doy-ee sǎhn]* waiting room

STREETS

ตรอก *[dtròrk]* sub-soy, lane

ซอย *[soy]* soy, lane

ถนน *[ta-nǒn]* road

TELEPHONE

บาท *[bàht]* baht *(unit of currency)*

เหรียญ *[rěe-un]* coin

ต่อ *[dtòr]* extension

โทรศัพท์ทางไกล *[toh-ra-sùp tahng glai]* long distance telephone calls

ตู้โทรศัพท์สาธารณะ *[dtôo toh-ra-sùp sǎh-tah-ra-ná]* public telephone kiosk/booth

โทรศัพท์ *[toh-ra-sùp]* telephone

สมุดเบอร์โทรศัพท์ *[sa-mòot ber toh-ra-sùp]* telephone directory

เบอร์โทรศัพท์ *[ber toh-ra-sùp]* telephone number

TIMETABLES

ถึง *[těung]* arrives

วันที่ *[wun-têe]* date

ออก *[òrk]* departs

น. *[nah-li-gah]* hours

เวลา *[way-lah]* time

กำหนดเวลาเดินรถ *[gum-nòt way-lah dern ròt]* timetable, schedule

TOILETS

บุรุษ *[bOO-ròot]* gentlemen
สตรี *[sa-dtree]* ladies
ช. *[chor]* men
ชาย *[chai]* men
ผู้ชาย *[pôo-chai]* men
ห้องน้ำ *[hôrng náhm]* toilet, rest room
สุขา *[sÒo-kăh]* toilet, rest room
ญ. *[yor]* women
หญิง *[yĭng]* women
ผู้หญิง *[pôo-yĭng]* women

Reference Grammar

NOUNS

GENDER AND ARTICLES
Thai nouns have no genders and there are no articles, neither definite nor indefinite. So, depending on context:

rohng rairm	means	the hotel or a hotel
reu-a	means	the boat or a boat

SINGULAR/PLURAL
Thai nouns use the same form for both singular and plural. So, for example:

pôo-chai	means	man or men
pôo-yĭng	means	woman or women
rót	means	car or cars

Frequently the context will be sufficient to make it obvious whether the speaker is referring to a single item or to many.

However, if you want to use the plural together with a number word, then Thai uses special counting-words called *classifiers*.

CLASSIFIERS

In English, when we want to count *uncountable* nouns like 'butter', 'cattle' or 'bread', we have to supply another word with the number. For example:

two *packs* of butter
twenty *head* of cattle
four *loaves* of bread

These italicized words which we have to supply for counting uncountable nouns are similar to Thai classifiers. However, in Thai, this system applies not only to uncountable nouns but to countable nouns too. So, for example, 'three cars' and 'three policemen' translate literally into Thai as:

cars-three-vehicles
policemen-three-people

The commonest classifiers for countable nouns are:

kon	people (except monks and royalty)
kun	vehicles
cha-bùp	letters, newspapers, documents
chín	pieces (of cake/meat/cloth/work)
dtoo-a	animals, tables, chairs, clothing
bai	fruit, eggs, leaves, cups, bowls, slips of paper such as tickets, documents
lêm	books, knives
lǔng	houses
lôok	fruit, balls
hôrng	rooms
hàirng	places

Uncountable nouns, like their English equivalents, are often counted by reference to the container in which they are stored or purchased. So food can be counted in 'plates', coffee in 'cups', beer in 'bottles' and so on.

When more than one item is being counted the order of words in Thai is:

noun + number + classifier

For example:

(noun)	(number)	(classifier)	
rót	**sǎhm**	**kun**	three cars
dtum-ròo-ut	**sǎhm**	**kon**	three policemen
mǎh	**sǒrng**	**dtoo-a**	two dogs
glôo-ay	**hâh**	**bai**	five bananas
dtǒo-a	**sǒrng**	**bai**	two tickets
bee-a	**sèe**	**kòo-ut**	four bottles of beer
kâo pùt gài	**sǒrng**	**jahn**	two plates of chicken fried rice
ba-mèe náhm	**sǎhm**	**chahm**	three bowls of egg noodle soup

When only one item is being counted the order of number and classifier is reversed:

For example:

(noun)	(classifier)	(number = 1)	
dtum-ròo-ut	**kon**	**nèung**	one policeman
măh	**dtoo-a**	**nèung**	one pig
glôo-ay	**bai**	**nèung**	one banana
bee-a	**koo-ùt**	**nèung**	one bottle of beer
ga-fair	**tôo-ay**	**nèung**	one cup of coffee

Frequently, however, Thai will simply omit the classifier and **nèung**. For example:

pŏm bpai gùp pêu-un
I'm going with a friend

is usually adequate instead of:

pŏm	**bpai**	**gùp**	**pêu-un**	**kon**	**nèung**
I	go	with	friend	(classifier)	(one)

There are a number of nouns for which the classifier is the same as the noun itself. For example, **hôrng** not only means 'room', but it is also the classifier for rooms. In such cases just the classifier is used with the number. For example:

sŏrng hôrng	two rooms
hôrng nèung	a room

Note how the word **nèung** is omitted in the following expression:

mee	**hôrng wâhng mái?** do you have a room?
have	free (question word)

Units of time and measurement follow the same principle. For example:

săhm wun	three weeks
sŏrng deu-un	two months
bpee nèung	a year

Other plural words such as 'every', 'all', 'many' and 'several' are also used with classifiers. For example:

pêu-un	**tóok**	**kon**	all my friends
friend	every	(classifier)	

kon tai	**lăi**	**kon**	many Thais
Thai people	many	(classifier)	

There is also a general classifier **un** which can be used when you can't think of the right classifier for an object. For example:

pŏm (chún) ao sŏrng un
I'll take two thingies *or* two of them

ADJECTIVES AND ADVERBS

Adjectives in Thai follow the noun which they modify:

For example:

bâhn lék	the small house
kon jon	poor people
ah-hǎhn pairng	expensive food

A peculiarity of Thai adjectives to the Westerner is that they also function as verbs. The word **lék**, for example, means both 'small' and 'to be small' and **jon** means both 'poor' and 'to be poor'.

So the above examples could also be translated as complete sentences as follows:

bâhn lék	the house is small
kon jon	the people are poor
ah-hǎhn pairng	the food is expensive

The Thai verb 'to be', **bpen** *cannot* be used with adjectives. It can *never* occur in sentences like:

she's kind	**káo jai dee**	(*literally* she kind)
it's red	**(mun) sěe dairng**	(*literally* (it) colour red)
I'm tired	**pǒm (chún) nèu-ay**	(*literally* I tired)
I'm thirsty	**pǒm (chún) hěw náhm**	(*literally* I thirsty)

DEMONSTRATIVE ADJECTIVES

Thai has three demonstrative adjectives which are used with a noun and classifier. Note the word order.

(noun	(classifier)	(demonstrative)	
pêu-un	**kon**	**née**	this friend
mǎh	**dtoo-a**	**nún**	that dog
rót	**kun**	**nóhn**	that car over there

ADVERBS

Adverbs occur after the verb as in English. In Thai there is no distinction between the adjectival and adverbial form as there is in English. The word **dee** means both 'good' and 'well'; **tòok** means both 'cheap' and 'cheaply'.

For example:

kon dee	a good person
káo tum dee	he does it well
ah-hǎhn tòok	cheap food
káo kǎi tòok	he sells cheaply

COMPARATIVES

The comparative and superlative forms of adjectives are formed by adding **gwàh** (for comparatives) and **têe sòot** (for superlatives) immediately after the adjective.

For example:

pairng	expensive
pairng gwàh	more expensive
pairng têe sòot	most expensive

To say 'more expensive than ...' use **pairng gwàh ...**

For example:

is it more expensive than this one?
pairng gwàh un née rěu bplào?

it's cheaper by bus
bpai rót may tòok gwàh

it's more expensive by train
bpai rót fai pairng gwàh

POSSESSIVE ADJECTIVES

There are no distinct possessive adjectives in Thai. Possession is marked by the pattern:

noun + 'of' + personal pronoun

The forms are:

my (*male speaker*)	**kŏrng pŏm**
(*female speaker*)	**kŏrng chún**
your (*singular*)	**kŏrng koon**
his, her	**kŏrng káo**
its	**kŏrng mun**
our	**kŏrng rao**
your (*plural*)	**kŏrng koon**
their	**kŏrng káo**

For example:

bâhn	**kŏrng**	**rao**	our house
house	of	we	

rót	**kŏrng**	**pŏm**	my car
car	of	I	

Often, however, the word **kŏrng** is omitted:

pêu-un	**chún**	my friend
friend	I	

gra-bpăo	**káo**	her bag
bag	she	

PRONOUNS

PERSONAL PRONOUNS

Thai uses the same word for both subject and object pronouns; thus whether we translate the pronoun *rao* as 'we' or 'us' will depend on its function in the sentence.

Thai has a much wider range of personal pronouns than English. To give just one example: a Thai man may regularly use at least half a dozen different words for 'I/me' depending on whether he is talking to his wife, his children, his brothers and sisters, close friends, colleagues at work and so on. Fortunately a foreigner can manage very well using the limited number of pronouns shown below.

pǒm (*male speaker*)	I, me
chún (*female speaker*)	I, me
dichún (*female speaker*)	I, me (*more formal*)
koon	you (*singular*)
tûn	you (*singular: formal use*)
káo	he, him
káo	she, her
mun	it
ráo	we, us
koon	you (*plural*)
tûn	you (*plural: formal use*)
káo	they, them

Often pronouns can be omitted altogether.

For example:

glùp	**bâhn**	**láir-o**	**doo**	**tee-wee**
return	home	already	look at	TV

In isolation, such a sentence is ambiguous, as we have no idea whether it is 'I', 'you', 'he, she, it, they' or 'we' who is coming home and watching television; in a real-life situation this would be apparent from the context.

Thais generally avoid using the pronoun **mun** (it), and sentences like 'it's very hot', 'it's raining' and 'it's a long way' are normally rendered as follows:

rórn mâhk	it's very hot	(*literally* hot very)
fǒn dtòk	it's raining	(*literally* rain fall)
yòo glai	it's a long way	(*literally* it is situated far)

Here are some more examples. The pronouns supplied in the English translations are not the only possible interpretations of the Thai sentences:

bpai	**nǎi?**		where are you going?
go	where		

mâi	**chôrp**		I don't like it
not	like		

òrk	**bpai**	**séu hâi**	he's gone out to buy it for you
out	go	buy for	

Most people can be addressed using the 'you-word' **koon**. The word **tûn** is reserved for people who are very obviously, on account of their seniority or prominence, to be regarded as being of superior status. Monks are included in this category.

If you know a person's name the polite and friendly way to address them and to refer to them is by using **koon** in front of their first name. For example:

> **koon mah-lee bpai năi?**
> (*speaking to Malee*) where are you going?
> (*speaking about Malee*) where is Malee going?

POSSESSIVE PRONOUNS
As with possessive adjectives there are no separate forms for possessive pronouns in Thai. Possession is marked by the pattern:

> 'of' + personal pronoun

mine (*of male speaker*)	**kŏrng pŏm**
(*of female speaker*)	**kŏrng chún**
yours (*singular*)	**kŏrng koon**
his, hers	**kŏrng káo**
its	**kŏrng mun**
ours	**kŏrng rao**
yours (*plural*)	**kŏrng koon**
theirs	**kŏrng káo**

For example:

> **nûn kŏrng pŏm (chún)**
> that's mine

> **nêe kŏrng koon rĕu bplào?**
> is this yours?

> **mâi châi kŏrng káo**
> it's not his

RELATIVE PRONOUNS
All relative clauses in Thai can be constructed with the same relative pronoun, **têe**, which means 'who, which, where'.

For example:

> **bâhn têe káo yòo**
> the house where he lives

> **pêu-un têe bpen kon tai**
> my friend, who is a Thai

> **rót têe káo séu**
> the car which he bought

VERBS

Thai verbs, unlike those in European languages, do not vary their endings according to the pronoun:

pǒm gin	I (*male*) eat
chún gin	I (*female*) eat
koon gin	you (*singular*) eat
káo gin	he/she eats
rao gin	we eat
koon gin	you (*plural*) eat
káo gin	they eat

Neither is there any change in the form of the verb to indicate tense. So, for example:

rao gin means	we eat
	we shall eat
	we ate
	we have eaten

Frequently the context will be sufficient for it to be clearly understood whether the verb is referring to events in the past, present or future. However, there are occasions when it is important to be very specific about time or sequence of actions. In such cases, Thai modifies the verb, either by adding a word in front of it, or after it.

The most common of these time-markers in Thai are:

FUTURE TENSE
The word **ja** can be placed immediately before the verb to indicate future time.

For example:

káo ja bpai séu kǒrng
he is going to go shopping

koon ja bpai doo mái?
are you going to see it?

PAST TENSE
(i)

The word **ker-ee** can be placed immediately before the main verb to express the idea of having done something at least once in the past. It also conveys the idea of 'used to (do something)' in English.

For example:

> **pǒm (chún) ker-ee bpai meu-ung tai**
> I have been to Thailand

> **pǒm (chún) ker-ee chôrp**
> I used to like it

(ii)

The word **láir-o** can be placed at the end of a clause or sentence to indicate that the action of the verb has been completed.

For example:

> **káo glùp bâhn láir-o**
> he has gone home

> **pǒm (chún) gin kâo láir-o**
> I've eaten

When the time context is specified or is otherwise obvious, these time-marker words are frequently omitted.

For example:

> **rao bpai bpee gòrn**
> we went last year

> **káo bpai bpee nâh**
> he is going next year

CONTINUOUS FORMS
The word(s) **gum-lung (ja)** can be placed immediately before the verb to indicate the continuous form of a tense.

For example:

> **rao gum-lung gin kâo**
> we are eating/we were eating/we have been eating etc

QUESTIONS AND ANSWERS

It comes as a surprise to most Westerners to learn that there is no single convenient translation of 'yes' and 'no' in Thai. The choice of the appropriate word depends on the question, so before asking questions in Thai, you not only have to learn the relevant question-word but also what kind of responses it might draw.

A simple statement can be turned into a question by adding the question word **mái** to the end of the sentence:

For example:

káo yòo bâhn	he's at home
káo yòo bâhn mái?	is he at home?
ah-hǎhn pairng	the food is expensive
ah-hǎhn pairng mái?	is the food expensive?

To answer 'yes' to such questions, you simply repeat the verb:

For example:

A: **káo yòo bâhn mái?**	is he at home?
B: **yòo**	yes
A: **ah-hǎhn pairng mái?**	is the food expensive?
B: **pairng**	yes

If you want to say 'no', you place the negative word **mâi** in front of the verb.

For example:

A: **káo yòo bâhn mái?**	is he at home?
B: **mâi yòo**	no
A: **ah-hǎhn pairng mái?**	is the food expensive?
B: **mâi pairng**	no

Another common question form in Thai, roughly equivalent to the English question-tag, 'isn't it?' or 'aren't they?' etc, is formed by adding **châi mái?** at the end of a sentence.

For example:

koon bpen kon ung-grìt, châi mái?
you're English, aren't you?

róy hâh-sìp bàht, châi mái?
it's 150 baht, isn't it?

This is a very useful question form to learn because it can be used for checking that you have made the right assumption, for example about prices, times of departure, and other important transactions.

A 'yes' answer to a '... **châi mái?**' question is simply '**châi**'. A 'no' answer is '**mâi châi**'.

For example:

sèt láir-o, châi mái? châi/mâi châi
is it ready?   yes/no

Also very frequently used by Thais, are questions which end in '**... rĕu bplào?**' which means roughly, '(are you) ... or not?'

For example:

> **koon bpai rĕu bplào?**
> are you going (or not)?

> **koon chôrp gin ah-hăhn tai rĕu bplào?**
> do you like eating Thai food (or not)?

In fact it is not quite so brusque as the English '... or not?' implies, but it does nevertheless demand a definite response. If you want to say 'yes', you simply repeat the main verb (i.e. **bpai** in the first example, and **chôrp** in the second); for a 'no' answer to this type of question, you say **bplào**.

Some of the other most useful question-words are given below, together with examples; note particularly the position of the question-word in relation to the sentence.

(i)   **a-rai** what?

> **nêe arai?** what's this?
> this what?

> **káo kăi arai?** what is she selling?
> she sell what?

(ii)   **tâo-rài** how much?

> **rah-kah tâo-rài?** how much does it cost?
> price   how much?

> **bpai chêe-ung-mài tâo-rài?** how much is it to Chiangmai?
> go   Chiangmai   how much?

(iii) **yung-ngai** how?

> **koon ja   bpai yung-ngai?** how are you going to get there?
> you   will go   how?

> **pah-săh   tai   pôot wâh yung-ngai?** how do you say that in Thai?
> language Thai say   how?

(iv) **(têe) năi** where?

> **koon púk   yòo (têe) năi?** where are you staying?
> you   stay live where?

> **rohng-rairm yòo   (têe) năi?** where's the hotel?
> hotel   situated at where?

(v) **krai** who?

> **koon bpai gùp krai?** who are you going with?
> you   go   with who?

> **krai bòrk?** who told you?
> who tell?

(vi) **gèe** how many?

> **séu glôo-ay   gèe bai?** how many bananas did you buy?
> buy bananas how many (classifier)?

NEGATIVES

Negative sentences are formed by placing the negative word **mâi** immediately before the main verb.

For example:

káo chôrp	he likes it
káo mâi chôrp	he doesn't like it
pǒm (chún) kâo jai	I understand
pǒm (chún) mâi kâo jai	I don't understand

It should be remembered that, in Thai, adjectives function as verbs, so **mâi** is placed immediately before the adjective. Remember that **bpen** *cannot* be used with adjectives.

a-ròy	it's nice, it tastes nice
mâi a-ròy	it's not nice, it doesn't taste nice
sa-nòok	it's fun
mâi sa-nòok	it's not fun
káo sǒo-ay	she's beautiful
káo mâi sǒo-ay	she's not beautiful
káo gròht	he's angry
káo mâi gròht	he's not angry

An exception to this rule is when the main verb is **bpen** (to be) and it is followed by a noun. In such cases the negative is formed by substituting **mâi châi** for **bpen**:

káo bpen pêu-un kǒrng pǒm (chún)
he's my friend

káo mâi châi pêu-un kǒrng pǒm (chún)
he's not my friend

bpen gra-bpǎo kǒrng koon
it's your bag

mâi châi gra-bpǎo kǒrng koon
it's not your bag

pǒm (chún) bpen kon ung-grìt
I'm English

pǒm (chún) mâi châi kon ung-grìt
I'm not English

THE IMPERATIVE (GIVING COMMANDS)

The imperative can be formed by adding **si** (pronounced 'sí', 'see' or 'sée') after the verb.

For example:

fung si	listen!
doo káo si	look at him
bpèrt bpra-dtoo si	open the door

Negative commands are formed by using the word **yàh** (don't) in front of the verb.

For example:

yàh gin	don't eat it
yàh bòn	don't complain
yàh kêe gèe-ut	don't be lazy

POLITE LANGUAGE

In English we can vary our intonation of the same sentence so that it can sound either abrupt or polite; in a tonal language, sentence intonation is not so flexible, and politeness has to be conveyed by other means. One way is to use a more 'polite' form of a particular word; thus both **gin** and **tahn** mean 'eat'. But whereas the former is perfectly acceptable among friends, it would be more appropriate to use the latter in more formal situations, or when addressing strangers, superiors or older people.

Another important way of signalling politeness is the use of polite particles. These particles are untranslateable words tagged on to the end of a sentence to perform much the same function as intonation in English. A male speaker will add the particle **krúp** to the end of a sentence to make it more polite, and a female speaker will add the particle **kâ**.

For example:

> **pǒm bpen kon ung-grìt krúp**
> I (*male*) am English

> **chún bpen kon tai kâ**
> I (*female*) am Thai

When asking questions, male speakers use the same particle **krúp**, but for female speakers, the tone of the question polite particle is high, **ká**.

For example:

> **koon mah jàhk nâi krúp?**
> where do you come from?

> **káo bpai nǎi ká?**
> where is he going?

The learner should make a habit of using the appropriate polite particle at the end of every sentence and question. (Note that particles have not been included in the phrases given in the English-Thai section, to avoid unduly lengthy entries.) As you become more familiar with the language you will learn when and to whom it is permissible to omit them without causing offence, but at the beginning it is wiser to err on the side of appearing too polite.

Finally, when addressing Thais or referring to them, remember to use the polite title **koon** in front of their first name, regardless of whether the person is male or female. (Surnames are used only for official purposes such as record-keeping, and Thais are never referred to, nor addressed, by their surnames.)

For example:

> **koon mah-lee bpai hǎh mǒr**
> Malee is going to see the doctor

> **koon sǒm-chai chôrp mái?**
> Somchai, do you like it?

TELLING THE TIME

The Thai system of telling the time divides the day into four sections of 6 hours, rather than two of twelve. Thus, 7 a.m. becomes 'one o'clock', 8 a.m. 'two o'clock' and so on, up until midday. The process is repeated in the second half of the day after midday and then, after 6 p.m., 7 p.m. becomes 'one o'clock', 8 p.m. 'two o'clock' and so on up until midnight. Each of the six-hour periods is known by a different name in Thai and this name is used when telling the time. The names are:

dtee	for early hours of the morning
cháo	for the latter half of the morning
bài	for the afternoon, together with
yen	for the early evening
tôom	for the hours from 7 p.m. to midnight

The twenty-four hours of the day are set out below; notice that the words **dtee** and **bài** appear before the number and that **dtee** and **tôom** do not occur with **mohng** ('hour', 'o'clock').

midnight	têe-ung keun	**midday**	têe-ung (wun)
1 a.m.	dtee nèung	**1 p.m.**	bài mohng
2 a.m.	dtee sŏrng	**2 p.m.**	bài sŏrng mohng
3 a.m.	dtee săhm	**3 p.m.**	bài săhm mohng
4 a.m.	dtee sèe	**4 p.m.**	bài sèe mohng
5 a.m.	dtee hâh	**5 p.m.**	hâh mohng yen
6 a.m.	hòk mohng cháo	**6 p.m.**	hòk mohng yen
7 a.m.	jèt mohng cháo or mohng cháo	**7 p.m.**	tôom nèung
8 a.m.	sŏrng mohng cháo	**8 p.m.**	sŏrng tôom
9 a.m.	săhm mohng chăo	**9 p.m.**	săhm tôom
10 a.m.	sèe mohng cháo	**10 p.m.**	sèe tôom
11 a.m.	hâh mohng cháo	**11 p.m.**	hâh tôom

Paradoxically, **hòk** ('six') **mohng cháo** is earlier than **hâh** ('five') **mohng cháo**. Sometimes, Thais count the hours from 8 a.m. to 11 a.m. differently and use the following sequence:

8 a.m.	bpàirt mohng cháo
9 a.m.	gâo mohng cháo
10 a.m.	sìp mohng cháo
11 a.m.	sìp-èt mohng cháo

Half-past the hour is expressed by adding the word **krêung** ('half') to the hour. For example:

5.30 a.m.	dtee hâh krêung
11.30 a.m.	hâh mohng (cháo) krêung (*cháo usually being omitted*)
4.30 p.m.	bài sèe mohng krêung

Minutes past the hour are expressed as

hour-time + number + nah-tee ('minutes')

There are no special words for quarter past the hour or quarter to, both being expressed in terms of fifteen minutes. For example:

3.25 p.m.	bài săhm mohng yêe-sìp-hâh nah-tee
10.10 p.m.	sèe tôom sìp nah-tee
9.15 a.m.	săhm mohng (cháo) sìp-hâh nah-tee

For minutes to the hour the word **èek** ('further', 'more') is used, followed by number + nah-tee + hour-time. For example:

8.45 a.m.	èek sìp-hâh nah-tee săhm mohng cháo
2.35 p.m.	èek yêe-sìp-hâh nah-tee bài săhm mohng
10.55 p.m.	èek hâh nah-tee hâh tôom

The 24-hour clock system is used in Thailand for formal purposes such as radio and television announcements, timetables and so on; the word **nah-li-gah** is used for hours and **nah-tee** for minutes. For example:

18.00	sìp-bpàirt nah-li-gah
20.30	yêe-sìp nah-li-gah săhm-sìp nah-tee

CONVERSION TABLES

1. LENGTH

centimetres, centimeters
1 cm=0.39 inches

metres, meters
1 m=100 cm=1000 mm
1 m=39.37 inches=1.09 yards

kilometres, kilometers
1 km=1000 m
1 km=0.62 miles=5/8 mile

km	1	2	3	4	5	10	20	30	40	50	100
miles	0.6	1.2	1.9	2.5	3.1	6.2	12.4	18.6	24.9	31.1	62.1

inches
1 inch=2.54 cm

feet
1 foot=30.48 cm

yards
1 yard=0.91 m

miles
1 mile=1.61 km=8/5 km

miles	1	2	3	4	5	10	20	30	40	50	100
km	1.6	3.2	4.8	6.4	8.0	16.1	32.2	48.3	64.4	80.5	161

2. WEIGHT

gram(me)s
1 g=0.035 oz

g	100	250	500
oz	3.5	8.75	17.5=1.1 lb

kilos

1 kg=1000 g
1 kg=2.20 lb=11/5 lb

kg	0.5	1	1.5	2	3	4	5	6	7	8	9	10
lb	1.1	2.2	3.3	4.4	6.6	8.8	11.0	13.2	15.4	17.6	19.8	22

kg	20	30	40	50	60	70	80	90	100
lb	44	66	88	110	132	154	176	198	220

tons

1 UK ton=1018 kg
1 US ton=909 kg

tonnes

1 tonne=1000 kg
1 tonne=0.98 UK tons=1.10 US tons

ounces

1 oz=28.35 g

pounds

1 pound=0.45 kg=5/11 kg

lb	1	1.5	2	3	4	5	6	7	8	9	10	20
kg	0.5	0.7	0.9	1.4	1.8	2.3	2.7	3.2	3.6	4.1	4.5	9.1

stones

1 stone=6.35 kg

stones	1	2	3	7	8	9	10	11	12	13	14	15
kg	6.3	12.7	19	44	51	57	63	70	76	83	89	95

hundredweights

1 UK hundredweight=50.8 kg
1 US hundredweight=45.36 kg

3. CAPACITY

litres, liters

1 l=1.76 UK pints=2.13 US pints
½ l=500 cl
¼ l=250 cl

pints
1 UK pint=0.57 l
1 US pint=0.47 l

quarts
1 UK quart=1.14 l
1 US quart=0.95 l

gallons
1 UK gallon=4.55 l
1 US gallon=3.79 l

4. TEMPERATURE

centigrade/Celsius
$C=(F-32) \times 5/9$

C	−5	0	5	10	15	18	20	25	30	37	38
F	23	32	41	50	59	64	68	77	86	98.4	100.4

Fahrenheit
$F=(C \times 9/5) + 32$

F	23	32	40	50	60	65	70	80	85	98.4	101
C	−5	0	4	10	16	20	21	27	30	37	38.3

NUMBERS

๑ *[nèung]* 1

๒ *[sǒrng]* 2

๓ *[sǎhm]* 3

๔ *[sèe]* 4

๕ *[hâh]* 5

๖ *[hòk]* 6

๗ *[jèt]* 7

๘ *[bpàirt]* 8

๙ *[gâo]* 9

๑๐ *[sìp]* 10

๑๑ *[sìp-èt]* 11

๑๒ *[sìp-sǒrng]* 12

๑๓ *[sìp-sǎhm]* 13

๑๔ *[sìp-sèe]* 14

๑๕ *[sìp-hâh]* 15

๑๖ *[sìp-hòk]* 16

๑๗ *[sìp-jèt]* 17

๑๘ *[sìp-bpàirt]* 18

๑๙ *[sìp-gâo]* 19

๒๐ *[yêe-sìp]* 20

๒๑ *[yêe-sìp-èt]* 21

๒๒ *[yêe-sìp-sǒrng]* 22

๒๓ *[yêe-sìp-sǎhm]* 23

๓๐ *[sǎhm-sìp]* 30

๓๑ *[sǎhm-sìp-èt]* 31

๓๒ *[sǎhm-sìp-sǒrng]* 32

๓๓ *[sǎhm-sìp-sǎhm]* 33

๔๐ *[sèe-sìp]* 40

๔๑ *[sèe-sìp-èt]* 41

๔๒ *[sèe-sìp-sǒrng]* 42

๔๓ *[sèe-sìp-sǎhm]* 43

๕๐ *[hâh-sìp]* 50

๕๑ *[hâh-sìp-èt]* 51

๕๒ *[hâh-sìp-sǒrng]* 52

๖๐ *[hòk-sìp]* 60

๗๐ *[jèt-sìp]* 70

๘๐ *[bpàirt-sìp]* 80

๙๐ *[gâo-sìp]* 90

๑๐๐ *[nèung róy]* 100

๑๐๑ *[nèung róy nèung]* 101

๑๐๒ *[nèung róy sǒrng]* 102

๑๑๐ *[nèung róy sìp]* 110

๑๑๑ *[nèung róy sìp-èt]* 111

๑,๐๐๐ *[nèung pun]* 1,000

๓,๐๐๐ *[sǎhm pun]* 3,000

๑๐,๐๐๐ *[mèun]* 10,000

๕๐,๐๐๐ *[hâh mèun]* 50,000

๑๐๐,๐๐๐ *[sǎirn]* 100,000

๗๐๐,๐๐๐ *[jèt sǎirn]* 700,000

๑,๐๐๐,๐๐๐ *[nèung láhn]* 1,000,000

ที่ ๑ *[têe nèung]* 1st

ที่ ๒ *[têe sǒrng]* 2nd

ที่ ๓ *[têe sǎhm]* 3rd

ที่ ๔ *[têe sèe]* 4th

ที่ ๕ *[têe hâh]* 5th

ที่ ๖ *[têe hòk]* 6th

ที่ ๗ *[têe jèt]* 7th

ที่ ๘ *[têe bpàirt]* 8th

ที่ ๙ *[têe gâo]* 9th

ที่ ๑๐ *[têe sìp]* 10th